# PSYCHOLOGY FOR TAROT READERS:

## PASSIONATE FIRE OF WANDS

Henadzi Bialiauski

First published 2023
by Rowanvale Books Ltd
The Gate
Keppoch Street
Roath
Cardiff
CF24 3JW
www.rowanvalebooks.com

A CIP catalogue record for this book is available from the British Library.
ISBN: 978-1-914422-50-8
ePub ISBN: 978-1-914422-49-2

# TABLE OF CONTENTS

# INTRODUCTION

Fire is the first and, perhaps, noblest element. It has a lot of passion, impulsiveness and militancy, which can manifest itself as creative impulses, falling in love, aggression or just as taking a proactive attitude. Psychologists who may stay far from occult symbolism nevertheless often use "fire metaphors" to help conceptualise things they constantly deal with in their work. The poetry of the elements is a common language that helps people of different world views better understand and empathise with each other.

Why should a tarot reader study psychology? Maybe it's simple curiosity. It is difficult to ignore psychology when a client talks about developmental crises, panic attacks, behaviour patterns or defence mechanisms. Even a mystic understands that these terms are relevant, even if they seem somewhat alien. And once you start to learn them, you inevitably begin to wonder how all these concepts from psychological science are presented in your own native esoteric tradition.

In 2020, I conducted a study, "Census of Tarot Practitioners", among Russian-speaking colleagues. This was a small survey, the purpose of which was to build a demographic model of the tarot community. How many of us are there? Who represents the average tarot practitioner? What books do we read? What decks do we use in our work? In the course of this study, it was discovered that the majority of participants had also studied psychology. Others noted that they were planning on getting a qualification in this topic in the near future. Our community seems to have a strong inclination towards integrating tarot cards and psychology.

But how should a tarologist approach professional psychological literature during independent study? These books are very complex, written in often incomprehensible language, and sometimes it seems that without a special dictionary, a tutor or a fully fledged university education, they are simply impossible to read. There are not enough works in which complex professional terms from psychology are explained in language understandable to the esotericist.

I confess that I did not immediately come to the idea of creating such a book. My first instinct was to use the classic format and explain the meaning of each card through a psychological lens. But the problem is that each card of the tarot is psychologically loaded in a completely different way. For example, one could write a whole book about the psychological side of the Empress, but hardly manage a couple of lines about Temperance. In my opinion, Temperance contains much more religious and mystical meaning.

Psychology is such a rich and diverse field that it is not entirely clear what information to give and what can be omitted. I would like to talk about psychosomatics, parent–child relationships, trauma, addiction, psychopathology and a host of other interesting topics. All this is difficult to fit into one book. Moreover, which perspective would I use: psychoanalytic or cognitive, behavioural or existential? All of them have their own traditions in psychology. It seemed to me that it would be more useful to introduce you to a number of such unique paradigms so that you can see the advantages and disadvantages of each.

I could talk about the meanings of the cards, or I could talk about the difficulties in the practice of tarot itself. I do not think that it is useful for a tarot reader just to tie a certain symbol to one or another psychological concept. Tarot schools, of which there are many today, do not often directly teach the rules of counselling, which is essentially what happens between the practitioner and the client during their work.

A separate topic is the formation of the professional identity of the tarologist. Like any specialist, the tarologist goes through several important stages and transformations, but in the tarot community, it is very rare to find postgraduate mentorship and supervision. As a rule, students learn the meanings of the cards and then they are simply "thrown into the water of practice", hoping that they won't drown when working with real people. I also wanted this series of books to contain my views on and experience of how a tarot practice should be arranged.

Of course, the tarot cannot be considered in isolation from general esotericism. And here, as my research shows, each tarologist has an absolutely unique picture of the world. Unfortunately, if a person of Western cultural background blindly and literally follows Eastern esoteric tradition, it might cause a lot of psychological damage.

I also wanted to draw attention to the psychological traps that the modern Western seeker of the supernatural often falls into.

So, what kind of book do you have in your hands? You are holding one of four books, each organised according to the same principle. If you look at the table of contents, you will see that the book is divided into three parts, each with the following sections:

**ZODIAC:** In my opinion, the court cards are the most psychologically loaded, especially the 12 cards corresponding to the signs of the zodiac. Not all tarot readers are accustomed to viewing Kings, Queens and Knights in this way. I have always promoted such an approach, since reliance on astrology in this matter provides an excellent way to differentiate these characters and prevent them from merging into one vague image. You will understand exactly how one Knight differs from another, and how cards of the same suit are similar or different. Also, court cards describe the character and therefore provide an excellent introduction to subsequent psychological topics.

**VIGNETTE:** A fairly large amount of material in these books is theoretical, so, of course, we need examples to accompany it. Case descriptions are very common in psychology, but they also look academic and boring. Therefore, I took the liberty of presenting practical examples in the form of fictional stories about an aspiring tarot reader, Emma, to whom certain clients come for consultations, each with their own problems and character traits. You will see a lot in common between the description of the sign of the zodiac and the corresponding court card, with the psychological portrait of the client who comes to the tarologist in each chapter. It is important to note that names and characters in this section are the product of my imagination, and any resemblance to actual people is just a coincidence.

**CHARACTEROLOGY:** Again, we build a bridge from system to system. We start each part by discussing character in an esoteric way, and here we will look at the psychological character type that most closely matches this description. Of course, there is no direct comparison between the zodiac and these classifications (of which, by the way, there are several in psychology). But you will see a lot of similarities, as well as understand how psychotherapists see each type of character, the reasons for its formation and its basic needs, as well as problems that this character type is likely to encounter in life. I will constantly make references to how this information can be useful in tarot consultations, so as not to go entirely into psychological topics. After all, this book is for tarot readers.

**CORE TERM:** As you read, you will notice that some important psychological terms are repeated over and over again. In each part of the book, one such term will be given a special section, with several examples to help you better understand it.

**THEORETICAL LECTURE:** This is the main theoretical section, devoted to some particular area of application of psychology. In this section, we will not be tied to a specific psychological paradigm but will consider the topic from a general perspective. The theory will not necessarily be related to the vignette, but I will give other examples of how to work with it in the framework of tarot consultation.

**USEFUL TERMS:** One of the objectives of this book is to prepare fellow tarologists for subsequent reading of and immersion into professional psychological literature. To do this, we need to understand additional terms. As with the core term in each part, I will provide a lot of useful examples that will help, if you wish, to firmly build these concepts into your working vocabulary.

**REFLECTION ON A PRACTICAL CASE:** This is a very important but often underestimated aspect of our work. The fact is that our work often does not end when a client leaves our office and we close the door behind him. We keep thinking about the case, how we worked, what exactly we missed, and clients often bring in topics that resonate very intimately with events in our own lives. In this section, we will return to Emma again to see how the client influenced her in the future, what thoughts the case prompted in her, what changes it provoked in her inner world and philosophy. Her story is a kind of multi-part novel exploring her growth as a tarologist, inserted into this series of textbooks. The goal is not so much to entertain; there will be no detective story or romance here. The life of a tarot reader is exactly the same as the life of any other specialist. It is much more important for us to track the formation of Emma's professional identity, as well as her inner philosophy.

**PRACTICAL RECOMMENDATIONS:** Now we will try to integrate theory and practice. In this section, we will consider what Emma did right and what she did not take into account. How does her work look from a psychological and psychotherapeutic point of view? What advice could we give Emma if we were to supervise her work?

**TRAPS AND DANGERS:** Again, this section will provide recommendations, but, in this case, they will not be directly related to Emma's work; they will be, instead, useful for any tarot reader. Moreover, this time we will look at the most dangerous and painful mistakes a novice tarot reader may make. In my experience, a lot of people fall into such traps, and for many it leads to serious internal torment. Some will even give up the practice because they see no way out. In this section, I hope I can suggest a way out of some common problems at work and keep novice colleagues out of harm's way. According to my observations, for some reason, this is very rarely taught in tarot courses.

**PSYCHOLOGICAL PARADIGM:** Again, this section presents a theory—this time, the last one for the part. As I wrote above, in psychology there is no consensus on this or that phenomenon or problem; there are multiple perspectives or paradigms. Tarologists are most often familiar with the Jungian approach but know nothing about other systems. In this section, we will briefly review 12 such paradigms and discuss how they are similar to and different from each other. This will later help you read professional psychological literature more easily, as well as strengthen your ability to consider a problem from different angles.

**ESOTERIC ESSAY:** This section takes us back to esotericism, but with a focus on its theoretical and ethical issues. We will talk about the problems that any practitioner faces, regardless of the system she practises. To be a tarot reader and at the same time not think about what esotericism is in general is, in my opinion, impossible. These esoteric essays will help you immerse yourself in serious world view issues that may concern any practitioner.

**PROBLEMS OF THE TAROT COMMUNITY:** A completely new topic, which is practically not described at all in tarot literature. Of course, here it is necessary to disclaimer that the basis of this section is formed by my research on the Russian-speaking tarot community, but something tells me that similar observations could be made across the world. Today, isolation is a myth. We are all very closely connected. Many will argue about whether the tarot community exists at all. Well, let's discuss. In parallel, we will touch upon a number of other important and pressing issues in the life of a modern tarot practitioner.

This structure is the same across all four books in this series. You can find the planned structure for the entire series at the end of this book. I hope this stimulates your desire and appetite to read more. You may want to buy other books in this series. Many topics are very closely intertwined, and I will often reference the other books in this one. And there are definitely some especially important points that I will repeat several times across the series. This is important when comprehending such a complex and unfamiliar topic.

But what about a tribute to tradition? In these books, I will provide a lot of new terms and words—so, what cards are they represented by in tarot? I have tried to take into account such questions but have approached them a little differently than might be expected. In all the theoretical sections in this book, the reader will see fairly wide margins, in which, alongside the relevant text, a card from the Rider–Waite deck is depicted. This card will best convey the essence of the paragraph opposite it. At the end of the book, in the appendix, you can find the Index, in which the cards are listed in the usual order for you, along with the page numbers of where each card is mentioned. This, if you wish, will allow you to group the information discussed according to the cards and their meanings, as is done in most books on tarot cards. I only use the Rider–Waite deck for two simple reasons: it is the most detailed, and most schools teach their students in this deck. I work with upright and reversed card meanings, although I know that not all tarot readers do this. If you have been taught to use only upright meanings, then those cards that I present reversed should be considered as shadow, excess or deficient meanings of the upright arcana.

Well, with this we can end the introduction and proceed to the first sign of the zodiac, Aries, and the Queen of Wands associated with it.

# PART ONE

# SECTION 1. ZODIAC

## QUEEN OF WANDS - ARIES

### *Upright Position*

With Aries, the zodiac is born. And like any birth, it is accompanied by a powerful energy impulse. This energy does not just flow in a powerful stream, as it will in the case of King of Wands, or dissipate into many small flickering lights, as with the Knight of Wands. Here, it rages, gushes furiously, and completely disables the ability to think clearly. Of course, this feature makes the Queen of Wands a very bright and attractive personality. She's glowing, exceptionally optimistic; her positive outlook on life is contagious. With her energy, she is able to inspire a huge number of people who, for one reason or another, experience deficiency, sadness or depression.

Most often with the Queen of Wands, this energy impulse is associated with some idea that inspires her. She is "all on fire" with it, unable to see anything else. A person may not eat or sleep at such moments because there is so much energy, and the future is seen as so bright and promising that it has nothing to do with ordinary, everyday needs. The idea is so attractive that it makes the Queen of Wands all-powerful. Nothing, absolutely nothing, threatens her as long as her gaze is riveted to this idea.

Almost anything can be such an idea, as long as it is honest, decent and noble. This is because the Queen of Wands is a card of the suit of Wands, which is associated with the element of Fire. Of course, Fire is perhaps the noblest element, if we are talking about the positive pole of its manifestation. What is a noble idea? Pick up a kitten from the street and put it in good hands. Give Grandma not just a birthday present, but something that will make her smile and perk up with enthusiasm. Or it can be more global: convince everyone around you to take care of the environment. Organise a protest against an unjust political bill. Anything, as long as it is honest, decent and noble. Most importantly, the idea should be able to infect others. Queen of Wands is just a conductor of energy, and she completely loses her own sense of "self" in this idea, just to bring this light to other people.

Of course, as a conductor of such a powerful stream, it is very difficult to suspect the Queen of Wands of deceit or lies. What's on her mind is on her tongue. This type is generally not characterised by strategy, as a concept. If there is a wall ahead, then there is only one route: accelerate and break through it with your forehead. It is out of the question to go around the obstacle, to compromise or to pause. This makes the Queen of Wands, on the one hand, a very honest person. But, on the other hand, there is a strong emphasis on assertiveness and activity, which cannot be interpreted as exclusively positive or negative. Everything depends on the context, but it is undeniable that the Queen of Wands does first and thinks later. The proverb "measure seven times, cut once" does not apply to her at all.

If we take into account all of the above, then we cannot expect manipulation from the Queen of Wands. Her mind doesn't work that way. As soon as one sits down and thinks about the details, the energy flow becomes thinner, and the inspiring idea fades. The Queen of Wands cannot allow this, and therefore, prefers eloquent sermons or direct pressure to manipulation. She definitely won't sit and calculate the strengths or weaknesses of her opponent.

Why should she manipulate others if the idea that inspires her makes her bold, strong, sacrificial and passionate? She will even suffer hurt, for a "just cause" and does not fear dying for one. Others, by the way, are afraid of her precisely because of this quality. She is impossible to negotiate with, impossible to intimidate and impossible to bribe because she does not think about herself at this moment; she is entirely driven by her idea. Is it possible to kill an idea? You can suffer for it, you can convey it to others, but what is the life of an individual worth when there is such an idea?

However, one important caveat must be made here. The Queen of Wands, unlike the King of Wands, never burns with one idea all her life. Her energy always flows in strong swings. When she lights up with energy, everything else in the world ceases to exist for her. But time passes, and the energy flow can dry up. Then, a new idea appears, and the Queen of Wands lights up as passionately as before. Interestingly, she no longer remembers anything about what she admired so much in the previous period. Now there is a new idea before her eyes, the old one no longer means anything. Or, at least, it's not that inspiring anymore.

Another thing is important: like the old idea, the new idea is also something honest, decent and noble.

This is an interesting feature of the Queen of Wands—being able to focus on only one thing at a time. The main thing to remember is that, in her case, this concentration is global.

*Reversed Position*

Any astrologer knows that there are no bad or good zodiac signs. We can consider every sign in a positive or negative way, or in a high or low octave. In the case of the tarot, we will talk about either a reversed card or the shadow meanings of an upright arcana. What does the reversed Queen of Wands give us?

In this case, we are dealing with a broken internal compass and a distorted ability to distinguish between good and evil. If in an upright position, the idea with which the Queen of Wands burns is always noble and honest—despite the not entirely subtle methods of its embodiment in the world—then, in this case, the idea may be completely vicious. But, it is important to understand that, in the eyes of the reversed Queen of Wands, it will still be an honest and noble idea.

A classic example is the idea of just revenge or persecution of dissidents. It seems to the reversed Queen of Wands that she is doing "a work pleasing to God", but, in fact, we are dealing with mania, blindness and simply monstrous stubbornness. The upright Queen of Wands is also stubborn, but somehow naively childish.

Here we are dealing with a cruel and fierce stubbornness and rigidity, which causes much suffering and trouble to everyone around.

The inspiring sermons of the upright Queen of Wands, when reversed, turn into ossified slogans. The poet turns into a propagandist with rather unpleasant rhetoric.

The problem is that the pressure and strength of the impulse in the upright version of this card does not decrease at all in its reversed version but, on the contrary, only increases. If in the upright version, the Queen of Wands will break through the walls with her forehead, then in the reversed version, she will walk on heads. The result justifies the means—the slogan of any Queen of Wands. In the upright version, this gives her a touch of sacrifice and passion, but in the reversed version, it makes her a really dangerous figure who does not shun any forbidden tricks.

As in the upright position, the reversed Queen of Wands also lives with energy fluctuations and changes of ideas. Only in this variant, periods of severe depression appear on the surface in the absence of a flow. The upright Queen of Wands usually switches easily and often does not regret the past. Reversed, depression can be long, severe and very dangerous. The fact is that, at such moments, she often becomes a victim of dangerous manipulators who can give her another vicious idea filled, at least somewhat, with energy. And the reversed Queen of Wands embraces it with all her passion, since it is simply unbearable for her to be without energy at all.

This is a very interesting aspect of this card. The Queen of Wands, like a child, has an extremely loose and unformed inner core. She herself does not know what she is nor what exactly she thinks on this or that issue. But, if in the upright position she is saved by an energy flow that ennobles her and "teaches good things" then, in the reversed version, when there is no flow, she experiences a feeling of personality breakdown. To experience such a "psychological death" is simply unbearable. Of course, she would prefer to join any adventure, even criminal and cruel, just to not experience this inner emptiness.

Both the upright and the reversed Queens of Wands do not tend to understand the nuances of the situation. This card can hardly be called subtle. The reversed Queen of Wands basically divides the whole world into black and white; either you are with her or you are against her. Subtlety is completely absent, as is the ability to distinguish the context of a given situation. Imagine what happens if the energy pressure is still powerful. Then, of course, such a Queen will not bring any creation into the world. She will become an exceptionally destructive character, often in the service of some skilled manipulator, such as the reversed Queens of Pentacles or of Cups.

There is one more aspect that needs to be mentioned, and this is the incredible speed of this character. If the Queen of Wands wants something, then, like a child, she wants it right now. She is simply unable to wait for the right moment and is tormented by this. Naturally, such haste only adds to the rudeness and blindness in her actions, forcing her to make gross mistakes. For such a Queen, everybody around her is "slow" and she alone moves at the right speed. Calls to sit and think cause her great irritation; she's already quite hot-tempered, and trying to restrain her with sound arguments only angers her more.

# SECTION 2. VIGNETTE

## EMPRESS TAKES OFF HER CROWN, CHAPTER 1

"Mum, let me call you back! I need to run." Emma carefully shifted the sofa cushions, trying not to drop the phone, which she kept pressed to her ear with her shoulder.

"Where?" demanded her mother, at the other end of the line.

"Work. The client is coming."

"Ah… This." Her mother sighed disappointedly, and then said with alarm, "What do you mean, 'is coming'? To your home? Do you let strangers into your house?"

Emma began to seethe with annoyance. It was always difficult to end a conversation with her mother. Emma's mum was simply insatiable, especially when something bothered her. And she could always find something to bother her, even if she had to make it up.

"Yes and yes, and—oh, he's here! I'll call you back."

"Your father and I will see you at the weekend. He wants to discuss something important with you. Do not forget!"

"Of course he does. Bye."

Emma hung up and took another look around her room. Everything was ready. A small but perfectly clean and comfortable study. Lots of books on shelves against the wall. Their multicoloured covers, illuminated by the morning sun, stood interspersed with small but beloved trinkets from esoteric stores. All this gave the room a library or museum-like atmosphere.

Several decks of tarot cards lay on a coffee table covered in black velvet. At the left corner of the table, there was a candle in a beautiful antique candlestick.

There were still ten minutes before the client arrived, and Emma wanted to do a short meditation to get herself ready, the way she'd been taught at tarot school, two years ago. You need to work in the right mood, and her mother, as usual, had managed to alarm her with that reminder of the upcoming conversation with her father. She needed to clear her mind and tune in to work.

Emma sat down in a chair, lit a candle, closed her eyes, and was concentrating on her breathing when the doorbell suddenly rang. She shuddered and opened her eyes sharply.

*Damn it! What a bad habit, arriving early!* she thought.

The bell rang again, longer and more insistently this time, and Emma went to open the door.

A young man of about twenty-five stood on the threshold. He had a dishevelled appearance, a shifty look and a slight trembling in his hands as if he hadn't slept in several nights. He looked like a marathon runner in the last kilometre of his long race: a mixture of total exhaustion and euphoria, when the finish line is very close, and all that remains is to push a little more. The guy seemed out of breath, as if he'd climbed to the sixth floor on foot, forgetting about the elevator.

"Are you Fred?" Emma asked.

"Yes. Fred. We… called up… I've come for a consultation… I didn't find the place right away… I drove around the area, looking for the right house… I found… Then I parked… You know, here on the way…"

Emma wanted to remind the client of her name, but the guy didn't give her a chance to put in a word. He spoke intermittently, like a machine gun firing in short bursts.

"I met a friend… not even a friend, but you know… studied together… mediocrity, but he's been very impudent… imagine, he got a job… yeah, really… he got it… his dad arranged… said that now they'll be raking it in…"

Emma realised that this verbal flow would not stop on its own, so she gestured for the client to come in. He flew into the apartment, not for a minute stopping shooting his words. It was very difficult for him to stand still. He circled around Emma's small hallway and would have gone on circling if she hadn't pointed in the direction of the study. Fred, without slowing down and without stopping, burst into the room like a fighter and, oddly enough, sat down exactly where he was supposed to. He fell silent, but his eyes entered a battle with an invisible enemy, frantically rushing from object to object.

Emma sat down opposite and picked up the cards.

Fred suddenly froze and stared at her. He looked worried, then confirmed Emma's guesses. "I didn't sleep all night. You said that I need to ask questions... I'm not sure how to ask... The question should be specific—or abstract? Or how to—"

Emma interrupted the guy, trying to sound as calm and reassuring as possible. She was used to seeing an anxious client in front of her; it happened in every other case. Either the client was concerned about the problem that had brought them to the consultation, or the procedure itself, which for some unprepared people caused simply awe. That was why Emma tried to dress as simply as possible and did not add emphatically esoteric elements to the decor of her study; she knew the process wasn't always easy for the clients. Fred was no exception. It seemed that he was about to choke on his own stream of words.

"I'll help you formulate the questions," Emma said, and smiled to relieve some of the tension.

"No! I'm ready!" Fred was obviously talking louder than he needed to. "Main question. Everything depends on it. When will I earn my first million?"

Emma always tried to start consultations with an atmosphere of benevolent indifference. On the one hand, she wanted the person across from her to be relaxed and cooperative, but on the other, she'd quickly realised in the first year of her work, that too much friendliness could relax some clients to a disgusting level of familiarity, so she tried to keep her distance for at least the first five minutes. She'd even learned to keep a slightly stern expression on her face so the client understood that everything was serious, all the while getting a read on who she was dealing with. As a rule, if the client cooperated, she'd take off her mask of severity and then communicate very warmly and openly. But this stranger opposite her did not inspire confidence, so she raised an eyebrow sternly, straightened her hair in a businesslike manner and began to lay out the cards.

Emma loved simple spreads. At school she'd been taught many more complex options for all occasions, but she'd gradually abandoned them. Complex spreads took a lot of time, so usually Emma would just draw a significator card and then lay out the deck in three piles, creating a row of three symbols. She could always extend the spread with additional cards if new questions arose or the client gave feedback on its interpretation.

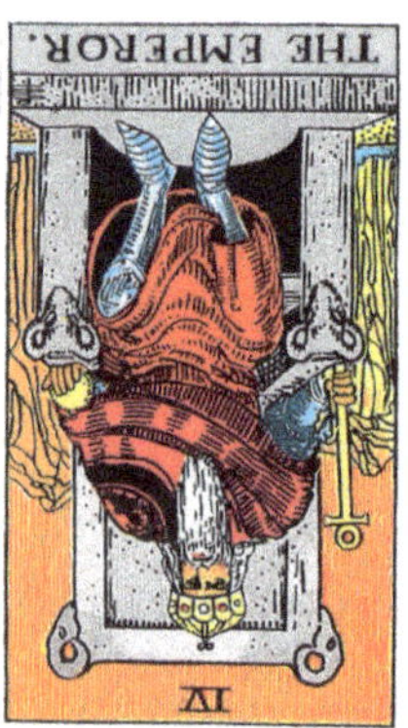

"I must warn you right away," Emma said, already realising that the client must be upset. "Tarot cards show time rather approximately. They show the essence of the situation more than specific time intervals."

Fred nodded nervously and was about to say something, but Emma beat him to it.

"Do you already know how you are going to earn a million? Do you have a business plan?"

Emma was stalling, preparing her client for a disappointing response. It was absolutely clear that, in this scenario, there was no question of "when?" at all; the tarot cards flatly denied Fred his desired million.

The cards fell as follows: the reversed Magician in the position of the significator spoke of the absence of a clear plan and a mediocre talent, and the Seven of Cups, as a card of dreams and fantasies, often empty and unrealisable, only confirmed this.

The reversed Emperor hinted at Fred's motives. Perhaps he wanted to impress his father, or some other male authority figure, with such a stunning financial success. Or maybe Fred's masculine self-esteem, which did not seem high, depended entirely on the money he earned.

Whatever the case, the outcome of the spread was absolutely clear: the Eight of Pentacles did not promise any million. It talked about ordinary work, monotonous and routine, which would bring ordinary prosperity. The Magician also suggested very high expectations, and Emma remembered from the training course that this arcana, astrologically associated with Mercury, often spoke of errors in thinking. Fred only thought that he was a great businessman. In reality, everything may be completely different.

"I do have a plan!" Fred blurted out. "I want to be a blogger and business coach—I'll sell success courses!"

Emma cursed inwardly. She knew a fair bit about business, thanks to her father, a successful businessman and editor-in-chief of a very influential business journal. Emma had received an excellent education. A prestigious university degree in marketing, plus a few extra courses in business, management and accounting. Just a gift for any office. At thirty-two, she'd already worked for seven years in various positions at several large companies, and she knew perfectly well what a real business was. And not to brag, but the projects she'd worked on were worth much more than a million. Looking at Fred, she understood that nothing like that could happen to the guy. That much was clear even without tarot cards.

*I wouldn't have hired you,* thought Emma, who had recruited and interviewed candidates for one of the projects. *If my father had interviewed you, he would have crushed you to the ground with a bang.*

But Emma caught on quickly. She was not her father and this wasn't a job interview or a competition. This was a tarot consultation, and Emma certainly didn't mean to severely frustrate her client.

Fred, still choking, was listing the online courses that he had signed up for, the business acquaintances he wanted to cooperate with, and the areas that promised fabulous money.

"I'm sorry to upset you," Emma finally decided, "but given the way you are today, you won't be able to earn the million you talk about. May I ask you, where does this idea to make a million come from? Can you say a few words about your father?"

Emma wanted to test her hypothesis. She could not help but take into account the reversed Emperor, which appeared in the spread. But Fred somehow heard Emma's question strangely.

"Not ready? Of course—that's what the courses are for. These are very successful people. It is important to stay close to them! They teach everything—"

"Will they teach you how to make a million?" Emma burst out. She worried that there was too much sarcasm in her tone.

In truth, she was beginning to feel sorry for Fred. It was absolutely clear that nothing would come of his dreams. However, she decided not to repeat the question about his father, since it was clear he was avoiding it.

"You know," Emma began cautiously, "perhaps not everyone needs to earn a million. Happiness is about more than just money. Tarot cards are a mystical system—not that mysticism and money are incompatible things—it's just that the answers often lie deeper than we think. Look at this card." She pointed to the reversed Magician. "This young man could represent you. What do we see here? On the table in front of him, we can observe the tools that he knows how to use deftly in his work. His posture, one hand up, the other down, suggests that he can transfer his ideas into real life—"

"Yes, it's me!" Fred exclaimed. His eyes lit up even more than before.

"But!" Emma continued. "You got it upside down. And this hints that you are using your talents incorrectly. You are not considering your strengths at all, but you're trying to be what someone else considers valuable. You seem to be trying to make a bicycle take off, although it was never meant to fly—it's not an aeroplane. But sometimes it's better to enjoy a superb bike ride and be happy than fly in an expensive business-class jet and—"

"Beggars' thinking!" Fred cut her off sharply. "You can't think like that—you'll never earn anything. All business coaches say so! You need to imagine yourself rich and successful today, then you'll attract the right people and money to you. Do you want me to send you a link to the coach I'm going to study with? I can if you want."

Emma's thoughts fizzled in her mind. In other circumstances, she would have been very angry, but there was something about Fred that didn't allow her to answer sternly and sharply. He was like a junior high school student who thinks he knows the answer and raises his hand with all his might so the teacher will notice him and give him the chance to prove himself. So, although his last remark could be considered rude, Emma restrained herself. Her sympathy for the client only increased. Of course, the guy still looked ridiculous. It was clear that he had no experience in business at all.

*Who filled your brain with that nonsense?* Emma thought to herself, but immediately pulled herself together. Fred was her client—he'd come to her for answers—and she needed to somehow help the guy.

"You know, I'm sure that money comes to people who do the right jobs for them. In my work, I have very rarely seen people who can earn equally well through literally all endeavours. It is important that their work evokes a response from within. When a person simply does what he loves, money comes to him naturally. Maybe we should take a look at different areas of business and see which one suits you best?"

Fred nodded.

Emma breathed a sigh of relief. Her tarot teachers had said that with difficult clients, sometimes it is better to simply rely on the drawings on the cards themselves. There is some magic in this. If the client, in connection with his questions, looks at certain symbols for a long time, they can miraculously change his mood. The cards seem to tune the broken piano of the client's mood.

Emma thought that if Fred now saw a long line of sad symbols, such as the arcana of the suit of Swords, he would calm down and begin to hear her better. Maybe then she could actually help him.

"What area would you like to consider first?" Emma asked.

"Business."

"Yes, but what kind of business?"

Fred hesitated. Emma was trying to lead him to the logical topic of being a blogger or business coach, which he himself had mentioned earlier, but he seemed to have already forgotten about it.

Emma patiently reminded him herself.

"Yes, let's see." He agreed with interest.

Emma gathered the cards, shuffling them carefully. And just as she thought, her hands revealed the reversed Magician again.

Emma was not at all surprised. In two years of work, she had already seen this more than once. It was one of the reasons she loved tarot so much—the cards were sometimes extremely eloquent. One sometimes got the impression that behind these symbols there were real, tangible forces—kind but strict—who wanted to help, but could not be persuaded to make a point that they did not want to. In this they are remarkably adamant. Repeating cards are especially important because they mean something valuable that the client does not want to realise. Emma showed Fred the reversed Magician and paused for a moment.

"Here. Look at this," she said.

"I see." Fred nodded and, for some reason, beamed with joy. "This means that I have a talent in this area!"

Emma shook her head.

"Note that the card is reversed," she hinted gently.

"Yeah," Fred agreed. "I'm doing everything right. There is talent. I need to develop!"

Then the real torture began. They moved from one profession to another. Emma understood that the tarot would not reveal the right line of work for Fred, and her strategy to confuse and cool his ardour with negative pictures on the cards clearly was not working. Whatever Emma said, Fred did a virtuoso feint with his ears and heard only what he wanted to hear, only what reinforced his faith in a future financial triumph. Emma didn't know how to convey to Fred the attraction of Eight of Pentacles from the first spread, the apprentice card that represents continuing to do the same—albeit tedious and boring—work, but at a very high level of accuracy. In the palette of meanings that Emma used, this card was not tied to any particular profession. It was not the field, but the format of work.

Fred, on the other hand, seemed to enjoy this "game" and willingly joined in. Emma gave up and obediently drew one card for each sphere.

They had been going through one sphere after another for half an hour. Each time, Fred began, with indestructible enthusiasm, to give examples of his acquaintances who had achieved significant financial success there. The cards turned out to be much more stubborn than the tarologist; they persistently denied Fred enchanting success, no matter what field of activity he chose. Emma had guessed right: she drew only Swords or reversed positive cards. However, the client did not see any negativity. In Six of Swords, he and his family sail on a luxury yacht. In The Hanged Man, he and his friends get into extreme sports and bungee jumping. Even Ten of Swords, which in the Rider–Waite deck is absolutely frank in its negativity, did not bother Fred at all. He saw Chinese acupuncture in this symbol and again began to talk about how he could build a business out of this.

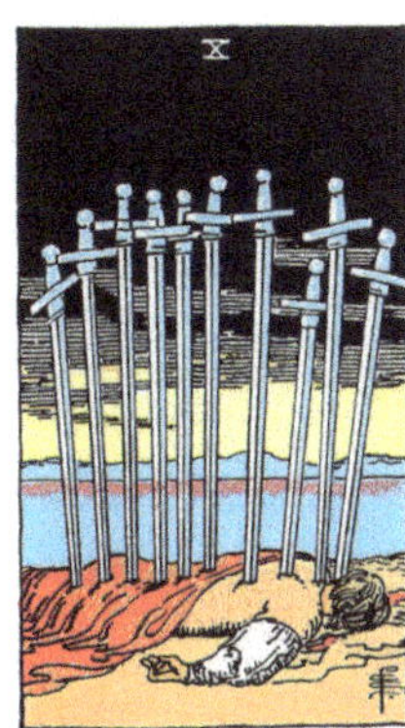


Emma was in a strange state. The client seemed to subordinate her to his own inner rhythm. She felt as if she had been put on a horse, which had bitten the bit and carried her off. It was impossible to jump off, impossible to stop—she could only cling convulsively to the saddle and gallop forward until the last forces run out. Fred made her feel weird. She felt like he was mocking her.

*Well, what the hell, acupuncture!* she thought. At such moments, she wanted to lean over the table that separated them and slap him. But this inner impulse crumbled into a steady inner voice in Emma's head, which repeated the same thing: *Forget it, it's useless.* She looked at Fred and wondered if he was high, or if he seriously believed in the nonsense that he was talking about.

Suddenly, on one of the questions, the client got the upright Chariot—a really positive card that could be tied to a specific profession. It depicted a triumphant figure riding a chariot from the city he had conquered. By no means would she tell Fred about this! It was a good thing he didn't notice it himself. Emma understood that, although the Chariot could represent a triumphant victory, in this context it simply denoted transport, and not triumph.

"Do you like to drive cars?" she asked Fred.

"I do," he said. "As a child, for some reason, I dreamed of being a trucker, to travel around the world."

"So, maybe logistics?" Emma suggested with great doubt, realising that this would be a poor compromise.

"No, the owner of an elite car showroom is better!" Fred's eyes flashed unhealthily again. "I have one friend… made a career in this field. He started out as an auto mechanic. Rose to a very high level."

Emma felt very tired. It was even becoming physically difficult for her to shuffle the deck and hold it out to Fred so he could cut it.

"Is there anything else you would like to ask?" she said, glancing at the wall clock that hung behind the client. There were still fifteen minutes before the end of the allotted hour, but Emma was ready to finish. In her opinion, further conversation was simply useless.

"When will I earn my first million?" Fred repeated. It was like the previous conversation had never happened.

Emma didn't say "never". Who was she, after all, to make such judgments? These were just cards. What if this guy really, contrary to all common sense, became a millionaire? In any case, Emma was not the person who should determine whether this was a sensible goal to pursue.

A whole series of consultations from the past two years suddenly flashed through her head: times when she had obviously misread the cards and then become very worried that she had not learned the meanings well, and then sadistically reread the notes over and over again for the next few days. The problem was not that these clients had complained to her—although this happened as well—providing accurate answers with the help of cards was so important to her that she got very upset every time she failed for one reason or another.

Fred vividly described his future luxury car showroom, and Emma recalled how her beloved grandmother, who had passed away about three years ago, gave her a Rider–Waite tarot deck on her eighteenth birthday. The same deck that Emma was now wearily shuffling, half-listening to Fred, but thinking about her own situation. She'd been very close with her grandmother. Emma's parents, especially her father, had never let her be lazy in her studies. And his efforts had paid off. The top student in her class, one of the top students in her university, Emma rarely disappointed him. "He's an important man!" her mother always said meaningfully, every time Emma didn't get what she always wanted from her father—admiration. He was proud of her, there was no doubt about it, but he was always proud of "future Emma", constantly and indirectly making it clear that with just a bit more work, she would actually achieve something, become someone and really delight him.

It usually looked like this: her father's friends would visit their home, so polished, as if they'd stepped from the covers of business magazines, but all of them somehow faceless. They always seemed to be fawning over her father, trying very hard to please him, or at least not accidentally ruin their relationship with him. When Emma grew up, she understood why: his journal was considered quite influential in business circles. Much depended on what was written in it, and being mentioned could be a good career opportunity. But when the guests and her father, having already drunk a little, switched to more informal communication, the same thing always happened, which disgusted Emma. He began to brag about her to his guests, constantly comparing her to the children of businessmen he knew. "She is so smart, so talented; she has such a future!" Emma was always embarrassed by such praise from her father. On the one hand, her usually over-strict and demanding father softened and simply began to sparkle with pride. But when she looked into the eyes of the guests, she did not see admiration in them at all. They either feigned nods, followed by disdain or envy, or had the greasy looks of men who had not heard of Emma's talents but were shamelessly examining her figure. Emma always blushed and wanted to sink into the ground at such moments.

The bar for success kept being raised, and Emma never saw true admiration in her father's eyes. "He's an important man!" her mother parroted when Emma's eyes filled with tears as a teenager.

Grandma had been completely different. She'd given the tarot cards to Emma secretly. She was not that fond of esotericism, but at that moment, she seemed to have guessed something about Emma that she did not yet know about herself. Grandma had waited until they were alone to take a velvet-wrapped tarot deck from her purse and hand it to Emma. The girl then did not even understand what fell into her hands. Together they opened the box and took out the cards. Emma looked at them with curiosity, and her grandmother suddenly took the Empress from her hands and said, "She looks very much like you!"

This arcana became Emma's favourite card. She didn't quite understand why. There was something in the image that attracted her very much.

Of course, Emma had begun to study tarot. First, by reading books. She'd been busy at work and didn't have enough time to study properly; her father constantly arranged work internships for her. Of course, if Emma were Fred, who was still sitting across from her now, describing the model-looking assistant who would supposedly be greeting customers at the entrance to his elite car dealership, she would've been overjoyed at these opportunities. She'd worked with very important companies and specialists, gained experience and earned good money. If she had really loved what she did, her career would've been incredible. But the fact of the matter was, she'd never liked it. She just did well. And the only pleasure she experienced was the release of tension when a task was completed.

When it became completely unbearable, Emma had secretly enrolled in a tarot school. The training lasted two years, and Emma learned a lot. It was then that she decided she would take up tarot counselling. She was tired of constantly talking about business plans, sales funnels, target audiences and other things of that kind. She was tired of not owning her time. She wanted to decide for herself when and how much she would work. But most importantly, she did not see any purpose for her in business. She wanted to be needed. In tarot, she felt it literally in the second month of practice. She got a client who, with her help, received an answer to a question that had tormented her all her life. They discussed at a consultation why the client kept entering relationships with men with whom she never managed to become happy. Perhaps Emma had just been in a good mood, but during that hour, she'd felt some indescribable inner delight. It was as if she had managed to put together a huge puzzle, and there was such understanding and gratitude in the eyes of the client that Emma thought: *This is it! I'm finally doing what I've always wanted to do!*

Her grandmother had been an ordinary nursery teacher and retired a long time ago. Somehow, she'd managed to see something in Emma that was hidden even from herself. She bequeathed to her granddaughter her apartment, in which Emma was now sitting with Fred. The accumulated funds from years of hard work in the business world had given her the confidence to take a sharp turn in her life.

Emma had moved into her grandmother's apartment, quit yet another company where her father had got her a job, and one evening "broke her father's heart" by announcing at a family dinner that she was leaving business and would now only deal with tarot. Her father stopped talking to her. If it were not the 21st century but the Middle Ages, he probably would have burned every single fortune-teller in the country out of a sense of impotent anger and resentment for such black ingratitude on the part of his daughter. A year later, he'd softened a little, and communication resumed, but he did not miss any opportunity to loudly mourn the death of Emma's brilliant career.

One extra good thing had come of it. She was no longer invited to dinners with her father's business friends. She no longer felt like a girl reading out poems for relatives who came for Christmas.

Fred seemed to be getting more and more heated, and Emma was getting more and more lost in her memories. Her hands automatically shuffled the deck, but she looked through Fred as he jumped across the clouds of the Seven of Cups, painting in colour how successful he would one day be.

Time was running out and Emma said, "We're almost out of time. Maybe you want to ask a final question?"

Fred came back to reality for a second and saw Emma in front of him. "What can I ask?"

"I do not know. It is customary to ask for advice," she answered languidly.

Fred obediently reached forward to cut the deck.

Emma revealed the Four of Swords. "Don't forget to rest and get enough sleep," she said. "You have such big plans ahead of you."

Although, to be honest, the card showed her own state at the moment more: terrible fatigue, as if she herself had just endured a serious battle, received injuries, and now wished that no one would touch her at all for some time.

Fred thanked her for the advice and fluttered out of her apartment as swiftly as he had flown into it. He was probably running to earn his million and look for a model-assistant for his car dealership.

Emma thought that she'd had so much planned for the day, but right now she didn't feel like doing anything. In the evening, she was meant to meet with friends, but she was thinking about skipping it now. For the moment, she wanted to be alone.

# SECTION 3. CHARACTEROLOGY

## THE MANIC CHARACTER

### Childhood

I am sure that you know, or have known, a child aged between three and five. Let's observe such a child and try to understand how they differ from an adult. There are a lot of differences, but I would first of all pay attention to totality.

For a child, everything happens in a 100 percent format. If they are happy, then they are 100 percent happy. If a child is angry, they are ready to destroy, to pulverise the object of their anger. If a child wants something, then they want it NOW, this minute, and they do not understand at all that it will take time to get it.

You must have seen this scene in a shop: a child likes a toy, but their mum or dad does not want to buy it. For some children, this feels like the end of the world. When such a child rolls on the floor, squealing and crying, it may seem to us adults that they are just manipulating us and their feelings are feigned. And this will be our huge mistake. The child's feelings are sincere, and they really live through the strongest suffering at such moments. A real catastrophe on a universal scale is actually happening in their life. This is not a joke.

Of course, I am not at all writing this to say that a child in such a state must definitely be bought a toy they like. It's just that an adult should understand that a child at this age is absolutely egocentric. Everything in the world happens because of them or thanks to them. I will give two very striking examples.

You have most likely seen young children eat chocolates. They become so deeply and totally immersed in the process that chocolate gets everywhere: on their hands, on their cheeks and chin, on their clothes. The child is completely captured by the taste of this sweet, its smell and the beauty of the wrapper.

Another, not-so-pleasant example is the divorce of parents. Many psychologists say that a child always considers themselves the cause of a divorce and blames themselves for this tragedy. Actually, this is not always the case. This happens only if the parents do not agree on who in this story will be a hero and who will be a villain. Today, many family counsellors teach parents this useful strategy. It is important that, say, a mother tells her child: "We are getting a divorce because Dad did something bad." And Dad, in turn, agrees with this version of events: "We are getting divorced because I did a bad thing." Then the child will not be tempted to take all the blame. But if Dad blames Mum, and Mum, in turn, blames Dad, the child is simply doomed to be the villain.

The child's psyche is not yet able to understand complexity and distinguish the shades of the situation. The world is exclusively black and white. That is why the child's psyche is still characterised by very primitive and early psychological defence mechanisms, for example, the total denial of anything that does not fit into his picture of the world. Children demonstrate this in play, at a slightly earlier age. If a child hides behind a curtain with half of their body sticking out but cannot see their mother, then it means that their mother does not see them either. That is: I see an object—it exists; I close my eyes and can no longer see the object—it is no longer in the world.

The child also has omnipotent control. This is how they see not only themselves but all the significant figures around them. I am a superhero! Mum is the most beautiful! Dad is the strongest! Grandpa is the wisest! By the age of six, if the child develops correctly, they will gradually get rid of this totality. But for now, the child really believes that they can make everyone around them do whatever they want.

The maturation and psychological development of the child involves a painful encounter with reality and a gradual deliverance from being egocentric. It's not that easy to do. It is good if, during a child's development, they encounter frustrations that are not so huge and total. The child's psyche can cope with them, or adults will come to his aid in time and share their own psychological resources. But this is not always the case.

Some children, unfortunately, face frustrations so strong and destructive that their psyche is simply unable to process the event correctly. Let's take as an example again, the divorce of parents, or even worse, the death of a parent. For an adult, such events are no less a disaster, but for a child, these experiences are multiplied tenfold. This is not just melancholy; this is the total disappearance of all colour from the world.

This is not just anger, but uncontrollable rage. This is not just a search for a reason or someone to blame, but often a total condemnation of oneself as irreparably bad and depraved. For example, "Mum died because I behaved badly, did not obey her and made her worry, so she got sick and died."

Here, let's immediately pay attention to one very important thing: a child in such a situation finds themselves facing a very difficult choice (if adults do not help them cope with the tragedy). The situation is coloured by such heavy feelings that they can either totally appropriate them into themselves or totally deny them. In the first case, we will get a depressive character, which we will talk about in detail in Book 3. But if total denial has worked, then there is a huge probability that we will get a manic character when such a child grows up.

The problem is that the power of this negative affect will not disappear. Starting from this moment, the psyche spends an incredible resource on not feeling sadness at all, maintaining the illusion that we are in control of everything, we can cope with all problems, we will always be cheerful and energetic, and we have only success ahead. And not just success, but, rather, triumphs—just in the spirit of an egocentric child.

## Adulthood

The manic character is always cheerful and optimistic. Feelings of sadness and powerlessness are so dangerous, even when mild and insignificant, that they are completely forced out of consciousness. If they feel even a slight hint of sadness, that state of total helplessness and awareness of their own badness, which the child decided to deny in childhood, will return. Of course, you need to spend a colossal amount of energy to constantly be in such an elevated state of positivity.

The manic character constantly lives "on the edge". They can neither eat nor sleep; they are totally absorbed by some great idea, which obscures all the negativity and protects against depression. Often, such people use various psychoactive stimulants to maintain this state of euphoria. By the way, all people suffering from any form of addiction have distinct manic traits in their character. We will talk about this in detail in Book 4, but you, I am sure, will have noticed that the drunken sea is knee-deep. The drug addict is often sure that he can quit at any moment, and the gambler is really completely absorbed in the idea that he is about to hit a solid jackpot.

Addiction is much more complex than this. Mania is just one of the traits of an addict. But even if there is no addiction, the manic character from the outside seems a little high. They have to be in constant motion. They'll joke nonstop, often completely inappropriately. They never stop, as it is simply dangerous for them to. Any stop or decrease in this frantic internal dynamic poses a serious threat to the psyche. Sometimes the following metaphor is appropriate: a manic person resembles a teenager who, closing their eyes, rushes headlong through a dark, dense forest full of dangers and horrors. They have only to open their eyes and look around, and reality will deal a crushing blow. It is better for them to simply run forward, eyes closed, imagining they are running through a field of flowers.

The manic character can overindulge in sex and drugs, to the point that they become dangerous. This is not necessarily the case; it is an extremely severe form of mania, which is already on the other side of the border between normal and pathological. Another pathological manifestation of this character is bipolar disorder.

The fact is, no matter how hard any person tries, reality catches up with them sooner or later. But for the manic character, this does not result in a simple change in mood. Here we are talking about periods of clinical depression, when a person simply falls into pitch darkness and cannot get out of bed in the morning, and, vice versa, periods of unbridled recovery, when life turns into a frantic race. These swings are happening constantly, and their power is the same as it was in childhood—absolutely total and all-consuming. Either totally in chocolate or totally in shit.

In the case of mentally healthy manic characters, things are not so bad. They'll just be a bit of a chatterbox. Everything described above is also applicable to them; it's just that the range of these swings is not so wide.

The manic character has many limitations in life, although they feel omnipotent. For example, such a person struggles to build long-term relationships. Getting close to another person is too dangerous, since it comes with the risk of separation and loss, and this cannot be allowed in any way, since a manic character is simply not capable of experiencing such a break. That is why it is much safer to dream of an ideal relationship, secretly fall in love, fantasise all possible plots from romantic novels, dream of an object of love, but in no case come close to this person in reality. In reality, such a relationship would quickly contradict their own imagined omnipotence.

By the way, sex maniacs do just the opposite. They might even forcibly involve victims in their mania, play out their "ideal" fantasy scenarios with them, revelling in the same egocentric power that is typical of young children.

## Need

As we will see with other character types, every person who interacts with another pursues some kind of psychological goal, which they may not be aware of themselves. What does a manic person do with other people?

They try to infect them with their mania. It is critically important for the manic character that the people around them share this enthusiasm and euphoria. The resources of one's own psyche are depleted very quickly, so someone else is needed who the manic character can feed on to fuel their tireless optimism and faith in their own omnipotence or triumph. And we must give them their due, they are exceptionally contagious and persistent in this undertaking.

Of course, ideally, a manic personality does not really need accomplices at all. They need a person of great emotional power who will face the real world with them and help them plunge into that horror of childhood loss that they never managed to work through. But this is so dangerous, so painful and unbearable, that it is easier, of course, to look for accomplices to their own Napoleonic plans.

# SECTION 4. CORE TERM

## TRANSFERENCE AND COUNTERTRANSFERENCE

In this series of books, we will discuss a lot of useful psychological terms. I have divided them into two categories. Some are just interesting, but will not necessarily arise in your work; you can work for years and never meet the clients these terms will apply to. But to the other group, I have assigned those concepts without which, in my opinion, it is simply impossible to work. They pervade our practice so entirely that they should be given special attention. The concepts of transference and countertransference are just such key terms, both in the work of a tarot consultant and a psychotherapist.

So, in psychotherapy, transference refers to when we experience feelings towards some unfamiliar person that are, in fact, being felt towards a different person from our past. Let's take an example. You arrive at your first lecture at university and you see the teacher. He's just started lecturing, but in less than ten minutes, you begin to feel great admiration for this person. He seems to you wise, expert, fair and caring. You are already fantasising about how you will become his favourite student, and how at the end of the course, he will celebrate all your achievements in a friendly way and say that you are almost equal to him in your talents.

Another not entirely pleasant example—a new employee has come to your office. The entirety of your interaction with her comes down to a couple of general meetings, seeing how she communicates with other colleagues, and perhaps noting the style in which she dresses, but you already feel a fierce hatred for her, and the strongest paranoia begins to unfold inside you. She wants to steal your position! She will certainly win all your friends over to her side. At the end of the year, it is she who will be promoted and not you, since people "like her" always suck up to the authorities and get what they have no right to. You are ready to just tear her to pieces. Too bad it can't be done without consequences.

Both of these examples illustrate a transference reaction. In the first case, it is a positive transference, in the second, a negative one. I'm sure you've already guessed what I'm talking about here. In the first case, we have a positive parental transference, most likely father-like, judging by the fantasies that arise. In the second case, it is a negative sibling transference, most likely to a younger sister, with whom rather painful competition unfolded in front of the parents in childhood.

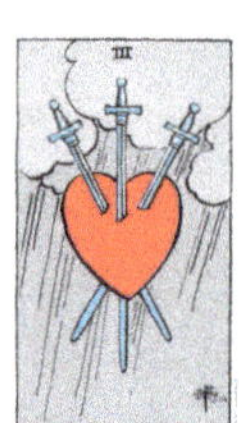

It is very important to understand the mechanism itself here. The fact is that not all of our past relationships have gone through a full cycle and ended ideally. As a rule, our psyche is overwhelmed with very emotionally charged fragments of relationships in which we really wanted something, but for various reasons we could not get it. But the problem is that these fragments continue to smoulder like dormant volcanoes, threatening to flare up again at any opportunity. They're like internal splinters that itch and haunt. As soon as a new person appears in our environment who, at least somewhat, reminds us of a figure from the past with whom we emotionally did not complete the relationship, our psyche begins to produce all the same feelings that we experienced then, attaching them to this new person.

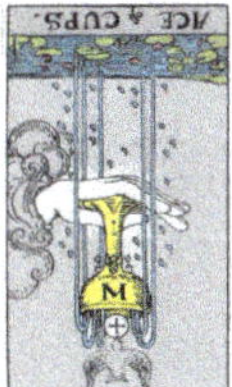


Transference is such a ubiquitous phenomenon that it's hard to find someone who has never experienced it in their life. A person in the present is delegated the role of some important character from our past, since we unconsciously want to extract that thorn from the inner world that continues to bother us. The difficulty is that transference is usually an unconscious process, and we do not understand why we feel the way we feel. However, there are several signs that will help us recognise it.

First, transference is always inappropriate. Let's go back to the examples above. Yes, perhaps the teacher is good-looking, perhaps he began to give a good lecture, but he has not yet given us a reason to feel admiration and dream of approval and praise. He is, in fact, no one to us yet. We could feel curiosity or perhaps sympathy for him, but certainly not admiration, this is an absolutely inappropriate feeling in this context.

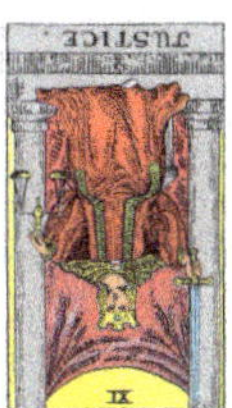


In the example with a work colleague, it might be appropriate to be wary, maybe a little annoyed, about the fact that a new employee behaves in some way different from what you are used to. But hatred, such a high degree of paranoia and the desire to tear her to pieces are inappropriate reactions in this situation.

Second, notice the intensity of the feelings in the transference. They are total, like the feelings of a child. This is absolutely not surprising, since we are usually transferring relationships with those people who surrounded us in our childhood: parents, the figure of mother and father; as well as siblings, our brothers and sisters. There are any number of family configurations, so these roles in childhood can be filled by other people. For example, a grandmother instead of a mother, an uncle or neighbour instead of a father, or classmates instead of siblings if there were no other children in the family. It is important to remember that transference feelings are always off the charts and seem alien to the psyche of an adult.

Third, transference feelings are always ambivalent. That is: yesterday the teacher praised me, and he was the best in the world, and today he praised my classmate, and I hate him. Such emotional swings, when we can experience different strong feelings for one person within the same day, are typical of the transference reaction.

And fourthly, transference is a very stable reaction. It is rather difficult to simply dismiss these feelings, even if you realise what is happening. It takes years to work through the transference in psychotherapy. Of course, there are techniques that can help you work with it, but even they do not allow you to quickly resolve the problem. The wildfire of feelings inside you is so huge that it takes time for it to discharge or go back into its capsule. They can also begin to dissipate once you actually get to know the transference figure. The differences then become so obvious that the transference is encapsulated again as the psyche loses the connection between the figure from our past and the person in the present.

Why is this term so important to us? The fact is that tarot clients are very likely to form a transference on you, usually parental. They may look at you not as an unfamiliar specialist who still needs to prove themselves, but as an already familiar figure from whom they need to get a certain reaction. But this is only half the trouble.

In response to a transference reaction, a countertransference reaction can form, and this directly affects how accurately we read the tarot spread. There are two types of countertransference. In the case of complementary countertransference, we begin to inadvertently feel for the client what his transference figures felt for them. That is, if the client had a mocking and depreciating mother, then in countertransference we may unconsciously deliver our interpretations in such a tone that they will sound mocking or sarcastic. It is interesting that, even if we ourselves are extremely caring by nature and dislike sarcasm, considering it cruelty, with this client we will begin to be tough and depreciating; we have been delegated a role and we unconsciously play it.

In the case of concordant countertransference, when we are with the client, we will feel the same way that they felt in childhood when with their transference figure. That is, in the same example with a mocking mother, we will feel extremely vulnerable during the consultation, even if this is not typical for us at all. It will seem to us that the client devalues our work, looks at us haughtily or with contempt, and our talent and experience seem only a trick of our rich imagination.

I hope you understand now why these terms are important to us as tarot readers. Here we are not talking about our psychological security, although we should not forget about it either, we are talking about the transparency of the process and impartiality in the reading of tarot symbols. Transference and countertransference, if they are not acknowledged, can absolutely ruin our work. As a result, the client is likely to be re-traumatised, their transference feelings re-encapsulated. And after such a consultation, we will have the feeling that we have participated in something extremely toxic. Imagine how psychotherapists, who deal with this every day, must feel. That is why, in any school of psychotherapy, one must begin by analysing oneself, otherwise working with clients becomes not only useless but also dangerous for all participants in the process.

# SECTION 5. THEORETICAL LECTURE

## PSYCHOSOMATICS

According to my observations, tarot clients are very fond of asking questions about their health, whether their own or their loved ones'. It is understandable, since this topic is of great concern to everyone. Moreover, most people try to avoid doctors. Clients either do not want to deal with the healthcare system of their country, or they are intimidated by the invasiveness of some medical procedures. The body is still a very intimate sphere of our lives, and we do not unnecessarily let strangers in there.

Tarologists respond to such questions in a very contradictory way. On the one hand, they all say out loud that they will not answer questions about the client's health with the cards. Such statements are heard in collegiate conversations, and my study of the practice of tarologists also confirms this. The topic of medicine is often considered forbidden, undesirable or ethically incorrect. But, on the other hand, if you analyse the numerous literature sources on tarot, you will notice that there is simply a huge number of symbolic correspondences between the cards and medicine. I am currently working on a large tarot dictionary in which the meanings of the cards, taken from numerous books, are divided by topic. The topic of anatomy, physiology and medicine is presented so widely and diversely that it seems time to write a separate textbook on medical tarot.

What does this mean? Many tarologists verbally renounce such work, but in reality, secretly from their colleagues, do they analyse the health of their clients? Let's try to understand this complex issue.

It is very important here to understand what exactly the tarologist looks at when asked a question about health. Most tarologists stipulate that tarot cards are not an X-ray machine, not a biochemical blood test, and certainly not an MRI. That is, we do not make a medical diagnosis; we talk only about psychosomatics. And here everything is completely confused, since when someone uses this "magic word", they put their unique meaning into it. On the surface, they mean the following cliché: "All diseases are from the nerves." Therefore, the cards will tell us what you're dealing with on a psychological level, and then it will become clear in what state your body is. This is a simple approach that allows tarot readers to stay out of doctor territory, while maintaining a certain compromise and not denying the client an answer to their question.

Now let's be serious. Scientific psychology and esotericism look at the term "psychosomatics" in different ways. Esotericists do not consider man and his nature in the same way as scientists at all. No scientist will talk about chakras, bioenergetics or the astral body. And for esotericists, including tarologists, these terms are a reality. In the esoteric picture of the world, any disease really originates in the subtle bodies of a person, and only then does it descend to the level of the physical body. "All diseases are from the nerves" can be translated to "all diseases come from problems with the subtle bodies". What are subtle bodies? These are a person's feelings, thoughts and value system, as well as their causal body, their balance of positive and negative karma. Indeed, any physical disease can be considered psychosomatic in this metaphor. But psychologists see the issue differently.

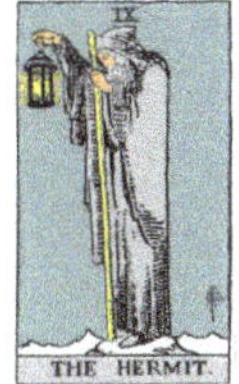

First, not all diseases are psychosomatic in nature, the therapist will tell you. From their point of view, only seven diseases can be safely called psychosomatic: bronchial asthma, ulcerative colitis, hypertension, neurodermatitis, duodenal ulcers, thyrotoxicosis and rheumatoid arthritis. In professional psychological literature, you can find these called "Alexander's Seven" or the "Holy Seven". Psychologists consider themselves scientists, and consequently, they will never call something psychosomatic unless it is empirically proven. Of course, this list may be added to with new discoveries over time, but so far, psychologists are in no hurry to declare any disease as psychosomatic, unlike esotericists.

In psychology, psychosomatics is considered to be the following mechanism. Let's imagine a child again, only this time, an infant who has not yet learned to talk. This level of development of the psyche is called preverbal, that is, before having learnt to speak. The child can verbally convey absolutely nothing to the mother, but communication between them, nevertheless, is in full swing. It's just that the child speaks a different language. It is the language of bodily sensations and symptoms. That is, instead of the child not yet having any personality, his body speaks, and it is very sensitive and fragile.

In this period, the role of the mother is huge. Her task is to tune in very finely to her baby and guess his condition from his bodily signals in order to satisfy his needs in a timely and correct manner. For example, the crying of a baby can mean a large number of things: the child is hungry, he is cold, he wants to be picked up, he doesn't want to be picked up. You can go crazy trying to solve these puzzles, but it's what the mother has to do. But that's not all. The mother not only has to guess and come to the aid of the baby in time, but she must also teach her child to verbalise his states over time. This is a long but extremely important process of translating states into words when the child is already learning to speak. A rich vocabulary should be formed inside him, connecting his feelings and states with words and phrases. If this process occurs correctly and at the right time, such a person will not be inclined towards psychosomatics in the psychological sense of the word in the future.

In cases when the mother, for whatever reason, did not cope, her child will become an adult who continues to lack words in their psyche for some of his states and experiences. That is, instead of their psyche, their body still speaks. A psychosomatic symptom is a message delivered by the wrong messenger; a person has no words to express their emotional condition, so the body helps its master to communicate with the world, like in the period of infancy.

Let's look at an example. Very often, skin diseases are referred to as classical psychosomatics. I don't think I'll be telling you anything new when I remind you how important touch is for a child. In psychology, there is a concept called "adhesive attachment"—the vital need for the mother to take the baby in her arms, where skin-to-skin contact occurs. Without confident, sensitive and careful contact of this kind, the child's psyche cannot develop fully. Let's imagine a situation where the mother did not cope with this task. She takes the child in her arms not when he wants it, but when she needs it. Moreover, she holds him incorrectly, perhaps shaking him. The child screams at the top of his lungs, while the mother becomes frightened and angry. Through this, her touch becomes, for a sensitive baby, like the touch of a red-hot poker. How can he, besides crying, convey to his mother that she has disrupted this act of communication? Of course, to give out a bodily symptom, in this case, a skin reaction.

An adult, of course, does not remember how he was picked up in infancy. But the body remembers it well, especially the skin. For such a client, problems will arise not only with bodily contact but with any contact that the psyche recognises as toxic. That is, he can react with his skin to depreciation, to indifference, to a very fast psychological approaching of the interlocutor. The problem is that these violations have remained at the preverbal bodily level, and the adult personality often simply does not have direct access to them.

In psychotherapy, work with psychosomatics is very long and complicated. The therapist, in fact, needs to complete for the client the work which the mother failed to do in her time. The therapist needs to tune in to, competently mirror and, finally, verbalise his client's state. This takes years of work because, let me remind you, we are dealing with a very deep level of the psyche. The client himself does not have access there, and he will not let the therapist go there right away. He would like to, but he won't, since all the mechanisms of psychological resistance protect this zone.

Who should generally diagnose a client with psychosomatics? Certainly not a psychotherapist, and definitely not a tarologist. This should be done by a medical doctor who has conducted all the necessary tests and did not find a physiological cause for the disorder. That is, the client must first examine his symptoms traditionally, and only then, when he is told that the problem seems to be psychological, should he seek help from a psychotherapist.

Doctors themselves sometimes do not understand how a psychosomatic illness is formed. They simply feel powerless and say, "This is psychosomatic" without explaining to the patient what this means. The patient hears: "Get out! I have no idea what's wrong with you!" And he still doesn't know what to do.

If a client with a real psychosomatic problem comes to you for a tarot consultation, then you can be sure that he has already exhausted all the possibilities of traditional medicine. He is desperate, but does not want to go to psychologists, perhaps because he does not trust them. It's easier to come to a tarologist. What if the problem could be solved by a miracle! Here, we are dealing with a huge ethical dilemma. The client has still come to the wrong address! It's not that you can't see the connection between a client's symptom and psychological problem with the help of the cards. But, within the framework of one single tarot consultation, you will not be able to "cure" such a client in any way. The best thing you can do is explain in a language understandable to the client what psychosomatics are and why he needs to go to a psychotherapist.

Today, to my great regret, there is literature containing tables in which certain bodily symptoms or even diseases are correlated with psychological problems. This is terrible because it reduces the problem to a dangerous simplification. As a result, the client hears the following: "Your right side hurts; you are angry" or, "Your left eye is watering; you are jealous." What is the disadvantage of such an approach? The fact is that if you're only working with such books to understand your symptoms, you do not receive the mirroring you need from a psychotherapist. These connections simply cannot be universal. It's like with dream books, which we will talk about in detail in Book 4. If you dream of a fish, this does not always mean that you will become pregnant. Instead, you need to explore what kind of symbolism the fish has in the unconscious of this particular person. And in each case, these associative links will be unique.

With symptoms and bodily sensations, the picture looks similar. Each person with colitis in their right side has it for their own individual and unique reason, and not necessarily because they are angry. And a competent specialist here will not hang a label, but will tune in emotionally to the client, will mirror them, and look for a unique and very accurate verbal formulation of this symptom.

So, what can tarot do here? It all depends on the client and the format of work. If you try to explore real psychosomatics with the cards, you will notice one very unpleasant effect. Suppose you are an experienced tarot reader, with excellent skill in interpreting and linking together various symbols. You never have difficulty finding the right words, and clients have often told you this in feedback. But if you immerse yourself in the study of a real psychosomatic symptom, you will feel as if an atomic bomb has exploded in your mind. All the words have disappeared, the mind has stopped, and you, normally so linguistically gifted, now can't connect two words, can't even think, because there is absolute emptiness in your mind. Well, welcome to psychosomatic countertransference! You have correctly tuned in to the client's situation—and you should be congratulated on this—but now you yourself feel either like a preverbal baby, who can neither speak nor think, or like the mother of this baby, who is tuned not to words but to guessing the state of her baby and doing something, not talking. After all, words will not help now.

I would like to add one more comment to this topic. We can only be competent mediators in this matter. Curing psychosomatic symptoms is not our area of work. We can only work with the client's resistance and unwillingness to go into serious psychotherapy, where they will really be helped. Of course, many people consider getting physically sick to be noble, while getting sick mentally is shameful and unpleasant, so many clients with psychosomatic problems are ready to go anywhere but the right address. It is definitely not worth playing along with this resistance to getting real, qualified help.

# SECTION 6. USEFUL TERMS

## Character – Accentuation – Psychopathy

I'm sure everyone has heard the word "character". We actively use this word in everyday life, even if we have not read a single book on psychology. Usually, we consider our "character" to be some stable structure of our inner world, which, in various situations, makes us react in certain ways. If we continue this line of thought, then we can absolutely correctly assume that character develops in childhood. During this period, each person is formed in unique conditions, surrounded by specific adults with whom they develop their basic behaviour patterns. But then there are quite natural questions: How many types of character are there? Are there good and bad characters? Can we change our character during our lifetime?

Psychology adds some useful details that help us better understand the topic. Yes, indeed, we all develop our character in our childhood. And if in numerous situations in our childhood we chose and perfected certain behaviours, then they become extremely stable elements of our psyche, forming the so-called landscape map of our inner world.

The psyche is extremely resistant to change. There are two reasons for this. First, any qualitative change in the psyche is such an energy-consuming undertaking that even based on the laws of conservation of energy, we will unconsciously choose the old and familiar, and not the new and potentially dangerous. Psychotherapists are well aware that the client will rather be ready to "habitually suffer" all his life than to "go into unfamiliar improvements". Secondly, qualitative changes are always a threat to the integrity of the individual. And this is not a joke, since we are all afraid of mental disintegration and death no less than we are afraid of physical death. If some element of our psyche, even if it is a pathological element, is the load-bearing structure of our entire internal organisation, we would rather die than give it up. That is why psychotherapists try to remember that any individual will always choose the best of what is psychologically available to them at the moment. From the outside it may seem that they choose wrong, and there are millions of other, better decisions they could have made, but it only seems that way to us.

Let us now try to answer the question of whether there are good or bad characters. In this series of books, we will consider a classification of 12 characters, each of which can manifest itself in a person to varying extents. Now, there's a very important aspect of this that we can better understand if we turn to astrology. Have you seen what a person's natal chart looks like? This is a schematic representation of the sky at the time of birth, which, like in a freeze-frame, depicts the positions of all the planets relative to the signs of the zodiac and relative to the diurnal rotation of the Earth. What do we see there? We see an absolutely unique picture, in which the planets are most often unevenly distributed throughout the zodiac. That is, the Sun, by which we are accustomed to understand that we belong to a certain sign, can be, say, in Cancer. But at the same time, it may be the only planet that fell into this sign. The Moon, Venus, Mars and Jupiter could, for example, have ended up together in the sign of Aries, which becomes very accentuated by this positioning. And at the same time, there will be signs in which there are no planets at all.

The following, correct conclusion follows: in any person there are all 12 signs of the zodiac, just in an absolutely unique individual proportions. One sign (or, according to some astrologers, three signs) will be leading, and the rest will be secondary. In the psychology of characters, everything is exactly the same.

We can talk about a radical or a leading type of character, but at the same time, a person will definitely have features of other types of characters; they will simply manifest these to a much lesser extent. If all 12 types were manifested in equal proportions in a person, we could say that person has no character, meaning not that they are weak or easily influenced, but that they cannot be classified. Opposite traits cancel each other out like bicarbonate of soda neutralises acid. Such a person is like a chameleon or a werewolf who is constantly changing. But this is from the realm of fantasy. In reality, we have the following: usually, a person has one or two leading radicals of character, and the traits of the rest will manifest to a much lesser extent. For example, a person may be a narcissist with some elements of an obsessive-compulsive nature. These are his main radicals. But this does not mean that oral or, say, antisocial behaviour models are inaccessible to him. They may be available, and here we move on to the next question of how sustainable character is.

Let's look at the example again. How do the following series of words correlate: "son – father – grandfather" and "daughter – mother – grandmother"? Analysing these series, we see that we are dealing with two parameters: gender and age. If you replace gender with "type of character", then the right thought comes to mind: the same character can manifest itself in us with varying degrees of intensity. Just as "masculinity" is most clearly manifested in the father, much less in the son, and quite differently in the grandfather; in the same way, for example, the manic type will manifest itself with different intensity in the case of the leading character, accentuation and psychopathy.

Here it is convenient to rely on the concept of adaptability. We will talk about narcissists in detail in the next part of this book, but for now let's imagine a situation. A person can certainly achieve a lot if he manifests healthy narcissistic strategies in his career, while at home with loved ones, relying more on strategies of an oral character, which we will consider in detail in the second book of this series. That is, character is context-oriented and flexible. Many strategies are available to a person, and he operates with them according to the needs of the situation. Of course, he has his most mastered and favourite strategies, but he is not rigid in them, and with the proper level of awareness he can vary them. These features then reveal themselves at the level of character.

Accentuation is a very vivid expression of one of the radicals in a person's character, which usually manifests itself during periods of development crises. For example, during the teenage crisis, it is common to talk about character accentuations. A teenager loses adaptability and mostly relies on only one radical, for example, schizoid. But the therapist will tell you that this is on the verge of normality. Yes, from the outside, teenagers sometimes seem like they're "legal crazy", but at this age, this is normal. And psychotherapists are in no hurry to diagnose pathology in adolescents just because they overly emphasise a certain character radical and do not use others. Yes, they are less adaptive, but the context forgives this. The same thing happens in an adult in certain situations, although psychologists no longer talk about accentuations here. For example, the mother of a newborn infant may exhibit accentuated oral character traits, but she does it adaptively, remaining within the limits of the mental norm. So does a teenager. They need accentuation in order to survive the age crisis. And as soon as the goal is achieved, the selected feature can be smoothed out to the level of a normal character.

But in the case of psychopathy, we go beyond the mental norm and fall into the field of psychiatry. The very word "psychopathy" is a bit outdated. Historically, people with a powerful antisocial radical in character were called psychopaths, and now in casual language, when we use the term "psychopathy", we mean a "personality disorder". Here we are dealing with a complete lack of adaptability. The whole character is built around only one single radical, and all other strategies and models are inaccessible to the person. We are not talking about a certain period in a person's life, like an age crisis; this person is always like this, and their life is not easy at all, since life requires much more flexibility than they are capable of.

My comparison of the signs of the zodiac with the characterological classification is not to be taken literally. Yes, in both cases we have 12 types, and there are some overlaps. But this does not mean that these classifications fit together like a key to a lock. I want to save you from automatically considering yourself paranoid just because you are a Capricorn. Everything is much more complicated. Leo, of course, has a slightly stronger narcissistic radical, but this does not mean that there are no histrionic, oral or, for example, manic Leos. We will talk in other books in the series about the dangers of such automatic diagnostics. This comparison acts as a didactic reference model that will help us notice things that have previously eluded our attention, understand our clients better and make better predictions. It is important that we do not start labelling.

## Organismic Valuing

In my opinion, this term is perfectly personified in the Major Arcana the Fool. In the image by Pamela Colman Smith in the Rider–Waite deck, we see a carefree young man who, with a bundle over his shoulders, walks with a dreamy look and approaches the very edge of the abyss. A white dog at his feet seems to be warning him against a possible fall, and the whole card looks bright and even enthusiastic.

Organismic valuing is the ability of a person to be in strong contact with his own nature, to feel all his needs, to be devoid of internal contradictions and conflicts, and to not worry too much about what others think of him. That is why the card is called the Fool. From the outside, it seems that the hero of the card is behaving really stupidly and unreasonably. But he is driven by some inner wisdom, which also protects him. This is the wisdom of a child who has not yet been conditioned by the society around him.

Not every person is able to answer the question of what they want. Or, what they want may not be their desire at all, but the pressure of their family or society, a cultural code that must be taken into account in order to be part of society. The Fool is an outsider, he is alone. But we cannot survive without other people, so we must follow the rules and norms of the group. And so the Fool personifies a very subtle, but extremely important compromise—to be yourself among others.

Our clients are often deprived of the quality of organismic valuing, or they have temporarily lost it, otherwise they would not come to us for a consultation. Not that we as outsiders, even having such a unique tool as tarot cards, know what our clients need better than they do themselves. But we can help them a lot in the search for this lost organismic wisdom. The client, as a rule, does not feel himself, and we can accompany him in search of answers to the question of who he is. Sometimes the client just wants to be given the sanction to be different from others, to be a Fool. Why not choose the esoteric, quite a marginal and foolish sphere, in order to get this sanction for uniqueness there?

## Acting Out

We will look at this term from two possible angles. On the one hand, acting out can be a defence mechanism in the client's life, and it can really be disturbing. But on the other hand, it may be a need with which a client comes to us for a consultation. In each case, we are required to have a completely different work strategy.

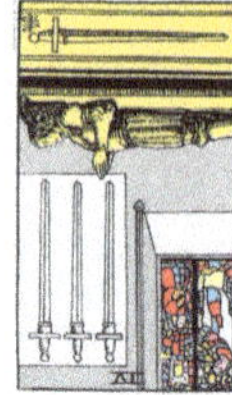

When we are dealing with a psychological defence mechanism, we are talking about a lack of awareness. The principle is very simple: not to feel. There are a great many examples of such a strategy, sometimes positive, but more often negative. Why be aware of your own anxiety and live it through when you can go to the refrigerator and eat another piece of cake? Why be aware of your impotent anger at your boss when you can come home and take all that anger out on your teenage child? Why deal with lingering excitement towards a woman on a first date, if you can immediately drag her into bed to reduce internal tension?

The client often asks: what should I do? But the trick is that sometimes you don't need to do anything. You just need to be in the state in which you find yourself and live through the feelings that accompany it. For many, this is so unbearable that they are ready to replace experience with action, which relieves internal stress only for a while, and only partially. Usually, the motivating need remains unsatisfied and, the next time, a new, even more powerful response will be required. We, as tarot consultants, can be helpful to our clients in this matter if, of course, they allow us. We can help them understand what need they are responding to, or what feeling they are afraid to experience. This can greatly advance the client as well as reduce the extent of their suffering.

The second angle of consideration of this term is that the client sometimes comes to us for a consultation only to express a certain powerful feeling. In this state, they do not need answers to questions or immersion in the depths of their inner world at all. It is simply important for them to reveal this feeling to another, to rent your psyche in order to cope with it. For example, imagine a client who is very indignant about something. They are so caught up in anger at the injustice that they don't care why it happened. It is important for them to get angry, to express this indignation to the full, because without this they simply cannot move on. Well, sometimes you have to forget for a while about your talent for in-depth interpretations and just listen to such a client. There is nothing else they can do in this state. But if you give them a safe space to act out like this, you will help them a lot.

## Zeigarnik Effect

This is a very simple term to understand, referring to the features of our memory. The famous Russian psychologist Bluma Zeigarnik discovered, around 1925, that unfinished actions are remembered much better than completed ones. This might seem obvious, but for us, as specialists working with the inner world of our clients, this effect is of great importance.

Why is our memory so selective about certain events in our biography? We can talk about the brightness of individual moments, which is why they are remembered. But you must admit that sometimes we have no memory at all of some events of great importance but have trifles very firmly entrenched. These are situations which were not completed. A focus of excitation arose in the psyche, but it was not properly discharged. We talked about this when describing the processes of transference and countertransference, another example of the impact of unfinished situations. The psyche continues to look for actors for the roles of significant figures from our past in order to satisfy the needs of a child that have remained hungry to this day.

You, as a tarot consultant, can quickly learn to notice this effect in clients. Where is the energy? What topics are the client charged with, and which ones are hardly of interest to them today? Should you scratch where it doesn't itch? According to my observations, if the tarot reader is sensitive to the client in this regard, the quality of the consultation greatly increases. I suggest asking the client to write a list of questions of interest to them before the consultation. In this way, they will illuminate the most highly charged aspects of their life today and will cooperate with you in your work.

And a last point related to this term. What do you think: should a client leave a consultation full or hungry? I don't think there is one answer for all tarot readers. I always try to ensure that the client leaves full but has not overeaten. I have colleagues who, on the contrary, end the consultation so that the client comes back. There are many ways to do this, but I don't think that is the right thing to do; I consider it manipulative. It is much better if the client receives from you exactly as much as they are ready to take away today, and that everything goes as if they are seeing you for the first and last time.

This is also necessary for the psychological safety of the tarologist. It is ideal for you to stop thinking about a client ten minutes after they leave. But if their "ghost" haunts you for another week after the consultation, then here it is, the Zeigarnik effect. Something has gone wrong in your work, and the psyche cannot complete this episode of your practice.

## Empathy

This concept is one that most people have heard of, but it is often confused with sympathy. They are not the same. Empathy is the ability to put yourself in another person's shoes and be AWARE of how they are feeling in a given moment. This does not mean that you should feel exactly the same and with the same intensity as they do. If you do, then you will not last long in such work.

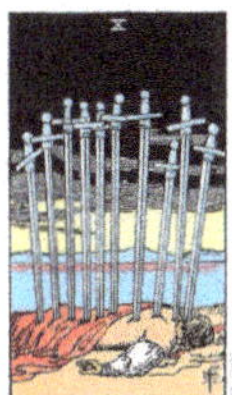

Imagine that a client comes to you in a state of acute grief. Someone very close to him has died, and the pain inside is such that he cannot cope with the experience. He's crying; he can't stop. If you completely merge with him and also start crying, the consultation will end; there is nothing you can do to help.

You may remember the situation from *The Addams Family* movie, in which Morticia Addams tells the kids in kindergarten a fairy tale. Of course, she turns it into a bloodthirsty horror story, which makes one child cry, and then, a chain reaction occurs: other children, seeing how the first girl is crying, all burst into sobs. This is not empathy. It's not even sympathy. It's just a psychological confluence. This is typical for children, since their own personalities have not yet been formed. Their borders are very permeable, so the confluence is easy and natural. Followers of religious cults also work like this, and they all feel the same euphoria when their leader preaches. Their personalities are also unstable and critical thinking is disabled. The crowd effect works the same way.

But there is another example. Often in films you will see a situation that has become a kind of cliché. The first character says; "I know how you feel", and the second angrily replies: "How can you know how I feel?" In fact, the first character is absolutely correct. They are speaking of their empathy. Their message can be translated as follows: "I understand that in your situation it is impossible to feel anything else, and I am not experiencing the same feelings now. But if I were you and had your character, your history, and got into the same situation, then I would feel the same as you do now. I'm not you; I have a different inner world. But such feelings are familiar to me, and I am ready to share them with you because now I am much more stable, and stronger."

Empathy is an extremely important quality for a tarot consultant, but it should not be confused with clairvoyance either. Of course, it has to do with general sensitivity, but it does not require supernatural abilities at all. There are people with a greater innate capacity for empathy, but it is a quality that can also be developed.

## Mentalisation

The last term for this part of the book. We have, in fact, already talked about it in the "Theoretical Lecture" section when we discussed the topic of psychosomatics. Here we will dwell on it a little more, since, in my opinion, it is also an extremely important concept for a tarot reader to understand.

Imagine the following situation: a client comes to you in a state of alarm. You start to investigate the problem, ask the client to tell you what exactly worries him, and he simply cannot do it. His anxiety is diffuse in nature. It envelops him in a dense, suffocating cloud, and he just cannot single out a specific object in all this fog that causes this feeling. You pick up the cards and begin to explore the state of the client. In the course of work, you understand that the client is, in fact, worried about losing a relationship with the woman he loves because it seemed to him that she was interested in their mutual friend. But this awareness is not available to the client himself, as it is dangerous for his self-esteem. Therefore, his psyche is in a state of diffuse experience.

Cards tend to show not only the problem but also the most obvious solution. And if you verbalise or mentalise diffuse anxiety here, by framing a vague and unconscious threat into a specific and clearly articulated fear, you will help your client a lot. Until an experience is mentalised, a person has no access to control it. When it gets a clear definition, then the client gains access to control.

Why do we sometimes like watching horror movies? They mentalise our existential anxiety or aggressive cannibalistic impulses. By watching these movies, we act these feelings out. This is an example of correct and healthy acting out. When our fears are embodied in the image of a real monster with specific abilities, appearance and habitat, our condition is relieved. Before, we were just in a dark room that we knew had a poisonous snake in it. Then the light was turned on, and we saw it. Now we know what kind of snake it is, how far it is from us, and how we can shield ourselves from it.

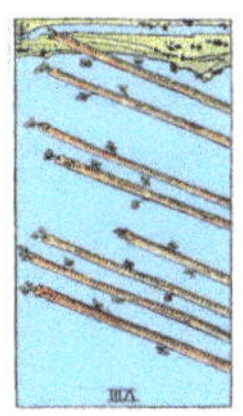

I think the metaphor is clear. We, as tarologists, can put into simple words what the client has long felt vaguely, but could not grasp. Now they have access to this experience. Of course, they can suppress it again—which, by the way, would indicate that we hurried our mentalisation. But if we did everything right and at the right time, then we rendered such a client a truly invaluable service.

# SECTION 7. REFLECTION ON A PRACTICAL CASE

## EMPRESS TAKES OFF HER CROWN, CHAPTER 2

By evening, Emma's mood had not improved. On the contrary, she'd fallen into some deep emotional hole. She'd had doubts before. She always justified it by reminding herself that she was a novice tarologist, and therefore, she must sometimes doubt. But this time it had hit her harder than usual. After working with Fred in the morning, she had basically begun to doubt that she could help anyone with her cards. Here comes such a character who already knows everything better than everyone. What could Emma say to him that would be helpful?

She should have been angry with Fred, but, instead, she was angry with herself, looking for flaws in her work, doubting that the job she had chosen was really so useful that she could devote her whole life to it. Maybe she shouldn't have quit her previous job. She could have still read cards as a secondary job or hobby. Why take such a radical step? And she'd also ruined her relationship with her father.

Still, she decided not to cancel meeting with her friend. She called a taxi and drove to a cosy restaurant where they often met. In fact, "friends" was a generous word. It was Greta, an eccentric lady of forty-eight who positioned herself as a witch, and her current protégé. Emma had never made any friends at the tarot school, where she'd studied for two years. It was mostly elderly ladies there, looking for an interesting leisure activity. Whenever she spoke to them, they'd lament about why she did not have a boyfriend and how she was still not married and did not have kids. Emma soon began to avoid these classmates. They seemed to her pathetic caricatures of her grandmother.

There had been some young girls at the school, most of whom dropped out halfway through. The rest of the class annoyed her very much. She thought them "shell-shocked by a rainbow"; men and women, of different ages and occupations, who emphatically adhered to positive thinking. They constantly repeated that "the world is love", smiled at everyone, and were cloyingly generous with compliments, which, to Emma, made them seem either hypocritical or mentally ill. She really didn't want to get close to them.

Emma had met Greta later on an online forum dedicated to esotericism. Emma had still had no friends in this area, and Greta seemed to be a very experienced lady, knowledgeable not only in tarot cards but also other esoteric disciplines. It wasn't that they were very close; it was just that Greta annoyed Emma much less than the rainbow shell-shocked followers of positive thinking.

Greta considered herself to be just a damn skilled witch. Everything about her appearance emphasised that she belonged to esoteric circles. All hung with amulets, like a Christmas tree, Greta always attracted the shocked looks of others. She liked to surprise people, and Emma liked to be in her company, because with her, Emma seemed to satisfy her own unfulfilled need for rebellion.

Emma doubted that Greta was her real name. The witch liked to boast that she came from an ancient Scandinavian family, sometimes speaking with a fake accent—although it sounded more Slavic than Scandinavian. There was always some young girl with Greta, like a magical familiar: a cat, an owl or a toad. The protégé was there today. Another young lady who looked at the witch with admiration and servility, and listened to her every word.

That evening everything was as usual. Greta and her protégé were already sitting at the table drinking cocktails. Emma came in, said hello, and joined the party.

"This is Sarah." Greta casually nodded towards her new protégé, as if hinting that now the adults would talk, giving her new student only the silent role of an admiring spectator.

"Nice to meet you," Emma said, and began to study the menu. She suddenly remembered that she had only had breakfast today, before her consultation with Fred. After that, she'd just had no appetite. Not that she'd managed to get hungry by the evening; she just needed to eat something.

"Something tells me you're not in the spirit, girlfriend," commented Greta. "Something happened?"

"Had a hard client this morning," Emma muttered in response.

"Emma is a tarologist!" Greta explained to Sarah, who looked obsequiously at Emma; an admiring *wow* flashed in her eyes. The girl froze with her mouth half open, obediently fulfilling the role she'd been assigned of a dumb admirer.

Emma decided she wasn't hungry after all, so she ordered herself a cocktail.

Greta wouldn't leave it alone: "What was difficult about this client?" she asked.

"Well..." Emma hesitated, not feeling the desire, or even the right, to tell the details. "This young guy asked how he could earn money."

"And you...?"

"I'm telling you—he won't get anything close to the money."

"I would make him an amulet for good luck!" Greta declared with theatrical pride. "There is one ritual, using runes, that works flawlessly."

Sarah again let out an obedient sigh of admiration, looking at Greta. Emma, on the other hand, was used to her friend's behaviour, so she habitually added, "And you would look at the second house in his horoscope."

"Yes, of course. Don't underestimate astrology!" The witch was outraged.

"You know I don't underestimate it. It's just that my heart isn't in it."

Emma had tried to learn astrology but didn't get very far; it just wasn't her way. Greta, of course, knew better.

Emma decided that she would not talk in detail about her work tonight. Greta was unlikely to support her. Most probably, she would lecture her with an arrogant air, like a senior colleague, and Emma definitely did not want that now. Instead, she turned to Sarah and asked a question, which completely broke the whole course of the usual theatre.

"What do you do?"

"She's a philology student." Greta gave an angry snort. "But let's hope that after her initiation, she will become a good witch."

"Do you really want to become a witch?" Emma asked Sarah, perhaps a little more sceptically than the code of friendship allowed.

Greta's face assumed such a condemning expression, as if Emma had asked something blasphemous, as if she had spat on an icon. *How can you ask such a thing?* And Emma decided that the best tactic would be to just stick to whatever topic Greta wanted to talk about and not argue. After all, she came here to have fun.

The waitresses, whom Emma already knew by sight, were very reluctant to approach their table. Greta consoled herself with the idea that they were afraid of her powers of witchcraft. Although it seemed to Emma, especially today, that they simply did not want to mess with crazy people. It seemed that they were casting lots to determine which of them would go to serve the coven that day. The waitress who was given this difficult chore looked very unhappy.

Greta talked all evening about a fellow astrologer who was now very popular on social media and took huge fees for consultations but, according to Greta, was not worth that much. The witch was very fond of gossiping and devaluing the work of colleagues. Emma did not participate in such conversations for the sake of gossip, it was just that, for her, it was the only way to talk with someone about esotericism, as well as find out the latest news. When it came down to it, Greta was indeed very well informed about the news in the community, and also a very well-versed esotericist herself. If it wasn't for her caustic nature, she really could have been an excellent teacher and source of knowledge. It was clear that she was very well-read.

The conversation didn't go well. Emma realised that she could not concentrate on what her friend was talking about, and after a couple of hours, she said that she was going home, since the day had been really long and not particularly joyful.

Greta did not argue and released Emma, saying, "Do not worry, dear! Clients can be such bastards."

Probably, it was because of this that Emma continued to communicate with this strange woman. No matter how she behaved, it was clear that she was still in tune with what was happening. Sometimes, like today, she even managed to somehow support Emma.

The way home was long. Emma deliberately chose to take the bus, as the long journey through the damp March, city streets suited her dejection more than a cosy and fast ride in a warm and dry taxi. Emma sat at the very back, where the light was less glaring and all the seats around were empty.

*What a strange world we live in!* thought Emma. In order to become someone, you must necessarily build someone else out of yourself, like some kind of endless narcissistic catwalk. If you want to be somebody, dress up! Put on someone else's tight clothes, distort your image beyond recognition, and only then, go on the stage! When you just want to be yourself, the world will do its best to show you that you are making a mistake.

Emma thought about Greta. She was a damn smart woman; she'd been in the craft for over twenty years and it seemed that there was no question she could not answer. They had been friends for almost a year, and Emma sometimes managed to see the real Greta behind this impregnable image of the Halloween Queen. There were moments when the spotlights above the stage went out, the audience dispersed, and she and Greta were left alone. At such moments, she was amazed at Greta's depth and wisdom. But as soon as she got under the spotlight again, the mysticism turned into a masquerade.

Emma was subscribed to Greta's social media. Her posts were simply impossible to read. Even Emma, with her little experience in esotericism, understood that the quality of the texts and photos could not be worse, but several thousand subscribers disagreed. Emma sometimes gave Greta advice herself on how to properly manage social media to get more followers. But here, for Emma, the esotericism ended, and business and sales began, while for Greta, it seemed there was no difference. Emma was sick of her being so indiscriminate.

Emma thought about Fred and fantasised about what the future held for him. She was absolutely sure that the guy had nothing ahead of him but a monstrous disappointment. Such an ending was inevitable. We all romanticise a profession until we plunge headlong into it. Such frustration and confrontation with reality can even be useful—but only if you've chosen the right sphere to throw yourself into.

Emma did not believe that you can choose the right profession at the age of eighteen. Rather, she believed that those who succeeded then were simply the unprecedentedly lucky ones. As a rule, the first choice of profession is wrong.

Fred was being influenced by too many factors that were confusing him. He lacked awareness of who he was and what made him unique—and then there was the pressure from parents, fashion and a whole bunch of other things. At closer to thirty than eighteen, he should've been able to think clearly and hear that thin inner voice telling him where to be and what to do. But it was not there. For many, this voice is silent all their lives.

The evening had relieved some of Emma's worries. She no longer had doubts about continuing to practise tarot, she just understood now what a difficult path she had chosen. It wasn't that working with people was difficult in itself—here the tarologist is in the same position as other professionals—the problem was that it was not clear how to develop and acquire her own style and opinion in this profession. She saw the same approach to business that she had been taught had infiltrated into the esoteric. She wanted to run away from it, to find a sphere that didn't have to work this way. But it seemed that everything had already happened: the market had captured the temple. She could easily imagine their conversation in the restaurant today in a completely different context as if they hadn't been discussing an astrologer colleague at all, but some competing business start-up.

Emma had been so fed up with it in her previous job in marketing that now she was seriously scared. She was very good at doing business, but that wasn't the problem. She'd gone into esotericism hoping that it would not be a business. It turned out that here you also need to think about subscribers, promotion, a product that will hook the largest target audience. These thoughts made Emma feel sick.

The bus pulled up in her street. Emma got out and wandered sullenly towards her house, past passers-by who'd wrapped themselves in raincoats, since night-time in March still had distinct winter notes. Approaching the house, she noticed a guy at the door with a large box of books in his hands. He tried to open the lock, but his hands were full, and he fumbled with the keys.

*Yummy!* The word flashed through Emma's head amidst this series of gloomy thoughts and doubts. She even shuddered; she did not understand to whom or what this word was addressed. Maybe she finally felt hungry. Or maybe the guy was cute. Emma brushed the thoughts away impatiently.

"Let me help you," she said to the guy.

He smiled back, thanked her and let her open the front door. They walked in together and headed for the elevators.

"What floor do you want?" Emma asked. The guy's hands were still busy with the box.

"Sixth," he replied.

Emma pressed the number six, not even surprised that they needed the same floor.

The guy asked, "You're on sixth as well?"

Emma nodded silently.

"We'll be neighbours, then," he said. "I'm moving into number twenty-five. My name is Tom."

"I'm Emma," she replied. "Do you like to read?" She pointed to the box overflowing with books.

"Very much," Tom replied. "Actually, I'll be renting one of the shops downstairs. I'm planning on making it a used bookstore."

Emma, unable to get rid of her gloomy mood, could not resist a caustic comment: "Bookshop? You can't do business with that today. Needs serious advertising to…"

She came to her senses and fell silent. Why was she being rude to this guy? This wasn't Fred at his consultation. With Fred, she hadn't dared to give him the truth directly, but here, without being asked, she'd decided to share her expert opinion.

"Well, this is not a business." Tom smiled. "It's a craft."

He didn't seem to be offended at all. On the contrary, he was glad that the conversation began between them.

The elevator door opened. Tom let Emma go ahead. They were ready to say goodbye, but then he asked: "What's your profession?"

"Marketer," Emma blurted out automatically and blushed all over.

Tom looked very surprised. "How strange. For some reason I thought you were a psychotherapist."

"Why's that?" Emma was surprised.

"I don't know," replied Tom. "You have such a look, as if you're not only digesting your own problems. I'm sorry, I shouldn't have—"

"No, no." Emma smiled for the first time since Fred had left. "I am very glad to meet you. If you ever need anything, I'm in number twenty-seven."

# SECTION 8. PRACTICAL RECOMMENDATIONS

## Practical Analysis of Chapters 1 and 2

Now let's take a closer look at Emma's work with Fred. The consultation itself was described in the second section, and you have just read the heroine's reflections after working with this client. If I may be allowed to take on a somewhat patronising, teaching tone, I want to say that for a tarot reader with only two years of experience, Emma did an excellent job. Here's why:

1. A good consultation starts before the client arrives. We see that Emma prepared a space for work. We will talk about this in more detail later, but from the description it is clear that the room, first of all, causes a pleasant feeling of comfort for the tarologist herself. She enjoys being in this room. She also made sure that the space does not emphasise esotericism. On this topic, among colleagues, there is no single point of view, but I like the way Emma thinks. If the client comes to the consultation excited, neither the room nor the appearance of the tarot reader should increase this excitement. Both the client and the tarologist should feel comfortable in their work. Any discomfort or excessive anxiety will negatively affect the reading of the cards.

2. Whether to meditate before work is the tarologist's personal choice. Here it is important to note something else, namely, Emma's attentive attitude to her own feelings. It is clear from the story that she wanted to do meditation because she was taught that way at school. However, here we cannot ignore the phone call from her mother, which roused her and interrupted the process, placing her in a non-ideal mental state for the consultation. Whether through meditation or some other technique, the heroine wanted to do everything right. She tried to leave her own

psychological material outside of the consultation. Perhaps in the future, as she gains more experience, she will find her own unique way of doing it. But her approach speaks, rather, about a neat and serious attitude to work.

3. Next is a very good point that I always note. According to Fred, he and Emma had a preliminary conversation. We don't know anything about how Emma arranged it yet, but this is something without which a psychotherapist, for example, will not work at all. Here we are talking about the so-called contract with the client, in which the essence of the process and the working conditions are discussed. So far, we know for sure that Fred was told to prepare questions. And this is a very good technique for a tarot reader because then, at the consultation the client will be more prepared, and not disoriented with no idea of what they want. It often happens that a client will come to a consultation and, out of excitement, completely forget what brought them there. If they have a prepared list of questions, it helps the tarologist a lot in their work.

4. Emma does not provide instruction. In Fred's case, it might not have helped at all, but I always believe that instruction is necessary. Perhaps Emma explained everything to the client during the preliminary conversation, but something tells me she didn't. This had to be corrected as the work progressed when Fred asked his first question and Emma had to explain that tarot can only show time intervals approximately. So, nothing was said about this beforehand. But, I repeat, every tarologist personally chooses the extent to which they want to instruct the client, and Fred is not the type of client for whom such instruction would be useful or necessary.

5. Let's make a very important point right away. In tarot, as in any other practice, there are simple and complex clients. In Book 4, we will summarise four types of dangerous clients. Fred, who is definitely a representative of the manic character, belongs to this group. I believe that Emma did everything right, but she made her decisions purely intuitively. If she had chosen a different strategy at some point in the consultation, things could have ended much worse. Of course, we cannot carry out psychodiagnoses of our tarot clients before they arrive, but there are some things that we can do. And Emma took them all into account in this consultation. Where does she demonstrate this?

6. Notice how Emma formulated her interpretations. She expressed them in the form of hypotheses. This is quite smart for two reasons. First, the client does not feel pressure, but rather an invitation to dialogue. That is, they are not sentenced to a certain rigid interpretation, but just how relevant something is has been made clear to them. This definitely allows you to work more accurately, both in the tarological and psychological sense. From a tarot point of view, we know that each card is overflowing with meanings. To choose the right meaning, we definitely need to rely on the unique context of the client. Therefore, we cannot insist on one interpretation at the very beginning, but we can offer options, waiting for the client to give their feedback. Then we suggest the next, already more accurate interpretation, and again wait for feedback. This allows you to come up with a unique and amazingly accurate interpretation of the spread, which will really be useful to the client. But this can't be done if the client doesn't cooperate and give feedback.

From a psychological point of view, this approach shows extreme competence. In the next book, we will discuss in detail the levels of personality organisation: neurotic, borderline and psychotic. Looking ahead a little, I will say the following: the classical method of interpretation affects all three types in completely different ways (it helps one, angers the second and destroys the third). You always need to start with hypotheses in order to understand who is in front of you. And only then can you move on to more daring interpretations.

7. I like how Emma intentionally kept her distance at the very beginning and did not immediately rush to save the client, pour out her love or provide the details of her own biography. In some cases, doing this can end very badly. In Fred's case, it would be simply useless. Emma, in my opinion, did the right thing. She tried to be serious and, as she herself thought, strict. In my opinion, she was not strict but emphasised the professional boundaries of the consultation.

8. Now, let's talk about Fred. I think you have no doubts that he is a man with a vivid manic character. All signs were obvious: his bodily condition, strong excitement, manner of speaking and not hearing anything. The concentration on only one super-idea, as well as the fact that he looked "insane". All these are beacons

that give us a hint about who is in front of us. I must say that the manic type does not often come to tarot consultations. But if they do, you need to be extremely careful, since you do not yet know how strong this manic radical is in them. There was one point in the consultation where Emma did absolutely the right thing. When she asked about Fred's father and he ignored her question, it was very good that the tarot reader did not push the client. I'll explain why:

9. In general, destroying the psychological defences of a client is an indicator of very rough work. First, it can be useless because, believe me, the human psyche is so arranged that you, most likely, will not be able to destroy with one phrase what it so desperately guards. You're wasting your time, and you're only pushing the client away. Secondly, we must not forget that the client does the best they can, with what's psychologically possible for them. And a good question arises: if you destroy a client's psychological defences, do you have something to offer them in return? It is important to remember here that saying, "Do this!" or, "Do as I do!" won't work at all. The client is not you, and no other person either. They cannot be offered the usual behavioural pattern, as it simply will not take root in their inner world. In order to offer something, one must first explore such a client for a long time, as therapists do. And having offered something new and destroyed the old defence, we still need to accompany the client for a long time, since they will not immediately learn the new behavioural pattern.

10. The third important point. Remember, we talked about "load-bearing structures" in the psyche; what if the defence you are now destroying is the last barrier before this person's complete psychological collapse? If so, the client just won't let you do it. It will seem to you that you are bringing him to awareness, and it will seem to him that you are killing him. Do not be surprised if you encounter a very violent and aggressive reaction. You probably do not have a panic button to call the orderlies, the police or your friends for help. Something tells me that with Fred, Emma avoided that risk. Imagine what would have happened if she'd tried to convince him that he was a dreamer who would not achieve anything. She may be right about this a thousand times over, but Fred is a man whose whole life revolves around his idea of financial triumph. Strong pressure on this issue, devaluation of this idea, ridicule or criticism—all this could have the effect of an exploding

bomb. Fred doesn't come across as having a highly adaptable psyche. His reaction to an attack on his dreams is very difficult to predict.

11. So, what do you do if a client brings mania to a tarot consultation? Here we must distinguish between two cases. Is the client manic only in regard to one question, while at the same time talking about other topics without such a strong emotional investment? Or is the client's entire inner reality concentrated on a single idea? In the first case, you can try to interpret this mania, but do so carefully. It is likely that the client simply does not notice how manic they are, and a correct analysis of their motives will allow them to better think over the movement towards their goal or even reconsider it. In the second case, you will probably feel how Emma herself felt: "Everything is useless." Such a client comes to you for energy, as their own batteries are about to burn out. It is useless to frustrate them, to call for awareness, to delve into motives. It is important for them to be reflected in your eyes and see interest and enthusiasm. This will keep them going for a while. But is it worth playing along with them here?

12. This is an open question. It all depends on the nature of the mania. In Fred's case, the situation is harmless; Fred does not harm anyone but himself. But there are times when mania involves other people, and here an ethical question arises. In the case of criminal mania, we, as specialists, have the right by law to violate the confidentiality rule and inform law enforcement agencies. But a client is unlikely to bring such a mania to a tarot consultation. Most likely, their mania will concern a career or a relationship. So, what to do?

13. Emma, in fact, did almost everything right. The only thing that she didn't take into account, costing her a good mood for the rest of the day, was the countertransference reaction. It was noticeable during the consultation how her mood deteriorated, and how she gradually fell into her own impotence. This often happens when in contact with a manic person. They are the pole of omnipotence, and in you they evacuate their impotence. The more grandiose their idea is, the more worthless you risk feeling after this work. At the other end of mania lies depression. If Emma had known this, she would have been able to separate herself from the feelings in the countertransference and would have come out

of the consultation more intact. In addition to the danger and unpredictability of a manic nature, in cases of severe disturbance, is the toxic countertransference when dealing with these clients.

14. What to do with a manic client at a tarot consultation? Survive. If you manage to understand what kind of person the client is even before their arrival, then it is better for you to refuse consultation. They don't need you. They won't see or hear anything you might say to them. They are hiring your nervous system to feed on your energy. However, if you do find yourself consulting for a manic client, it is very important to remember the following: the client in their mania absolutely does not care whether you are a tarot reader, a store clerk or a roommate. Imagine that you are stuck with such a person in an elevator. That would be torture. Just like in an elevator, in a tarot consultation with a manic person, your task is to get out of the situation with minimal damage. This says nothing about your competence as a tarot reader; you are generally absent now, as a tarologist. Believe me, there will be many more clients who will really benefit from you. Thank God that real manic clients very rarely come for consultations.

# SECTION 9. TRAPS AND DANGERS

## Absence of Preliminary Instruction

Now we will talk about a topic for which I am disliked by those fellow tarologists who believe that tarot cards and psychology are incompatible, who insist exclusively on a mystical and magical tradition. I understand them perfectly, but I continue to argue with them because I think that in this matter, they help themselves a lot, but harm the entire tarot community in the eyes of "ordinary" people, our clients.

Work with the client begins even before they come to us for a consultation. The client heard about us somewhere. Perhaps we were recommended to them by their friends or acquaintances who we've previously consulted for. But it is very important to understand the following: the client does not understand at all where they are going, what exactly will happen there, or what they, in fact, are paying money for. A tarot reader is not like a dentist, which every person has visited at least once in their life. This is a specialist in a field that is absolutely unknown to most people, shrouded in many false myths, and with no standard practice agreed upon by tarologists.

Fans of esoteric shows and hoaxes always benefit from such a situation. The client sits opposite, like a rabbit in front of a boa constrictor; ropes can be twisted from them, since they have entered a territory where they have no power at all—the tarot reader has all the power, and some simply revel in it. From the point of view of specialist/client relationships, a very unpleasant, unethical thing is happening in this situation, which could come back to haunt the tarologist and cause serious problems.

The point is not that the client needs to have "what tarot is" explained to them. Now I will say aloud a very seditious thing: no tarot reader knows for sure how to answer this question. Every tarot reader has a vision of what they do, no matter how much they differ from their colleagues, and a rule of good etiquette, in my opinion, is to convey this information to the client in understandable language.

I myself always involve two systems in my work. My consultations always use tarot cards and astrology, plus my psychotherapeutic training. One thing I always do, and I always teach to my students, is to begin a consultation with a preliminary instruction or briefing (if it's the client's first reading). I have a prepared speech that I always make. It only takes three minutes, but in my experience, it insures the tarot reader against a huge number of problems in the future.

First, I ask if the client has had similar consultations before, with tarot cards or astrology. Even if the client says that they have, I continue like this:

*"Let's start with the description of the procedure itself. All practitioners work in their own style, so it is important to clarify how this is going to work at the very beginning. So, we will work together in a dialogue. You will ask me prepared questions, and I will first lay out tarot cards for them. Tarot is a certain symbolic language, and my task will be to translate for you the answer from this symbolic language into a human one. You will then ask me the next question, I will give the next answer, and so on. At the same time, I will definitely check your horoscope, to make sure there are no discrepancies between what the cards show and what astrology says in your case. Although these are different systems, if we use them together in relation to your situation, they begin to correct and complement each other; we will receive more accurate information.*

*"It is important that you also be active, interrupt and correct me. This is because you always have the last word, not the cards or the stars.*

*"And one more important point. I believe that the tarot cards and the horoscope show the present moment. Of course, there will be a certain forecast for the future, but these things are quite fluid. Therefore, if something is revealed that you do not like, you definitely do not need to be scared. Rather, you will need to explore the situation more deeply and choose the direction that suits you. That is, we will not talk so much about tough predictions of fate, but more about orienting yourself in today and choosing the best direction for you."*

Why is this needed? In fact, such instruction is of great importance. First, you explain to the client the very essence of the process, talking about the role they are assigned within it. That is, you immediately indicate that the client should actively participate, since the quality of your interpretations depends on this. Plus, you give them the main role in the final decision. The client often does not know what to do with the information they're given. What even is the nature of this information? A verdict of fate, a view of the Higher Forces on his life, or just an opinion from the outside, albeit with the use of a mystical tool? With this speech, I return responsibility to the client. What final decision he will make, what choice he will make, is entirely his responsibility, not mine.

I also designate with this speech my criteria for competent consultation. I prioritise. First the present, then the future. That is, if a client wants to get an error-free and one-hundred-percent-accurate forecast, then they came to the wrong specialist. There are colleagues who have their priorities set differently. I believe that the predictive potential of tarot cards does not work that way. The accuracy of predictions is about 75 percent, according to my research. And there is always the risk of error. I am here in order for the client to better understand their situation, to clarify the circumstances of the choice that they face, to calm them down psychologically so they can CHOOSE FOR THEMSELVES.

Personally, I like to talk with the client on an equal footing, and it is precisely this equality that I covey with the help of this initial instruction. From practical experience, I can say that clients are very grateful for such an approach. It relaxes them from the very beginning because they understand that they will not be intimidated by something they do not understand anything about. They get back that share of power and responsibility that they lost while walking towards me. And they also understand that in working with me, no one will encroach on the principle of Free Will. This is extremely important because no matter how vulnerable they are, Free Will is a basic value that no one has the right to deprive them of.

The text of the initial instruction can be anything; it depends on what meaning you yourself put into your work. But it is important that you and the client tune in on the same wavelength and see the process more or less the same. This will help to ensure that you're a good match for your clients and they're a good match for you. It's good if you have a website that has some information about you and how you work. Customers like to read something in advance before they come to a consultation.

# SECTION 10. PSYCHOLOGICAL PARADIGM

## THE PSYCHODYNAMIC PARADIGM

Here is a topic on which I could write really a lot. If I do not stop myself, we'll end up with a whole separate book, and we do not have such a goal. All we need to understand is that psychology is a land of polyphony, which means that the same phenomenon or problem can be considered from the point of view of completely different theories. These paradigms, or perspectives, for analysing or explaining a problem, are associated with specific psychologists and their schools, as well as with specific techniques for and methods of how a psychologist should work with their client's problems.

It must be understood that one paradigm is not at all better or worse than others. Historically, they often appeared as a criticism and addition to the previous dominant paradigm. But at the same time, the old schools did not disappear. It's just that now practitioners have a wider choice of how to consider and work with a particular problem. There are a lot of paradigms today. In this book series, we're just going to take a very quick look at how one paradigm differs from another. We will definitely not go deep into theory, otherwise we will completely break away from the topic of tarot cards. Our task is to grasp the main metaphor of the paradigm in order to learn how to look at the problem from different angles.

At the end of the book, you can find a small list of useful psychological literature. These are professional books written in serious language, and you won't find a hint of tarot cards in them. But I hope that after reading this series, these books will become more accessible to you. In fact, if a practising psychologist read this series, he would not find anything new for himself from a psychological point of view. Perhaps he would even feel annoyed, since here I try to overexplain obvious things.

There are books in this list that are very useful for understanding the difference between various psychological paradigms. Authors often take one practical case and run it through all paradigms, showing how a psychoanalyst, a gestalt therapist or a cognitive-behavioural psychologist would work with a given patient. I repeat that all these paradigms are equally good, and any practising psychologist has an idea of them. Though they studied, most likely, within the framework of only one paradigm, this does not mean that they cannot use the techniques of a nearby school. Moreover, it often depends on the client and their problem. For example, with a midlife crisis, the existential model works better, and with phobias, cognitive psychotherapy gives a faster and more stable result.

So, the psychodynamic model. We consider it first for a reason. Sigmund Freud, its inventor, founded psychoanalysis and made great breakthroughs in psychotherapy in his time. All subsequent paradigms have appeared as criticisms of his approach. He is an extremely complex author, but now we will try to understand the main essence of his theory.

According to Freud, a person is driven by only two main impulses, instincts or drives—Eros (the instinct of life, sexuality and pleasure) and Thanatos (the instinct of aggression, destruction and death). These instincts are so basic that they are inherent in absolutely every person. But, if they are manifested freely, society will disappear very quickly, since the instant realisation of instincts will lead to the extermination of each other. Therefore, in the course of life, a person learns to restrain these instincts and find the right form of expression for them.

Freud also said that the human psyche can be viewed as the sum of conscious and unconscious elements; the unconscious takes up a much greater portion of the psyche than the conscious. Freud proposed the following topographic model of the psyche: id, ego and super-ego. The id is the unconscious part of our psyche. It is in it that all the instincts and desires that want momentary realisation are located. The super-ego is also often an unconscious structure, containing social taboos and moral restrictions that prevent these instincts from running at their full potential. And between the id and the super-ego is our ego—a certain social compromise between instincts and morality. The ego is our conscious part, which we present to the world around us.

So, what is psychodynamics? The main idea is that the components described above are not in a static condition. There is a constant struggle going on between them. Impulses from the id rush out of the unconscious because they want to get satisfaction, but here psychological defence mechanisms come into force. Their task is to protect the ego from certain impulses. Why is this needed? First, not all of these impulses are harmless. As we discussed above, their instantaneous and unrestrained discharge could create total chaos. Secondly, they threaten a person's self-esteem. Sometimes it is dangerous to be aware of what is rushing out of the id. A person can be much less attractive to themselves if they become aware of their own desires. And thirdly, the id is a total timeless chaos, while the ego, in turn, is always chronologically and clearly structured. A complete breakthrough of the id into consciousness can simply sweep away the ego like a tsunami sweeps away everything in its path, and then the personality simply disappears.

The following metaphor is convenient: ego is a city next to a huge, turbulent river (id), which is separated from the city by a strong dam (psychological defence mechanisms). But the problem is that this wild river (id) is the only source of water for the city (ego). You can't completely cut yourself off from it. It is necessary to take water from it so as not to destroy the dam.

Psychodynamics just speaks of this complex homeostasis or balance between desires and prohibitions, between impulses and morality, between the conscious and unconscious parts of our psyche. At different stages in a person's life, different events can occur in this difficult confrontation.

Freud also said that man goes through various stages in his development. He distinguished oral, anal, phallic, latent and genital stages. They are so-called because the instinct of pleasure in the child at each of these stages is associated with a certain part of his body. Freud has been criticised very seriously because he wrote about sexuality and childhood, but it is important to understand that Freud is not talking about adult sexuality here at all. He spoke of the pleasure principle, which is certainly present in infancy. The oral stage is so named, for example, because the infant's leading pleasure is associated with breastfeeding. At any of these stages, fixation can occur, which subsequently gives very important traits to the character of a person in adulthood. The incorrect realisation of a child's need and the balance of pleasure and prohibition is precisely that unfinished situation that a person will unconsciously realise all his life, since it, being highly abstract and symbolic, permeates his entire psyche.

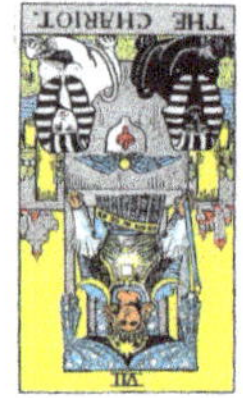

In other words, within the framework of the psychodynamic paradigm, psychological problems are a violation of this unsteady balance between the id, ego and super-ego, and are not necessarily recent. That is why psychoanalysis is an extremely long process of immersion in the unconscious, lasting for many years. The training of a real psychoanalyst is very difficult and requires the mandatory passage of one's own analysis. Behind the scenes, most non-psychoanalytic therapists generally accept that long-term psychoanalysis, thanks to deep immersion, produces real qualitative changes. It not only develops the client's mindfulness tremendously but also helps resolve very basic internal conflicts. The psychoanalyst takes a long and careful approach to that unique moment when a surgically accurate interpretation can be offered to the client. After that, the client experiences an internal catharsis, a psycho-emotional discharge of great power, which produces subsequent qualitative changes in his inner world.

Of course, the psychodynamic paradigm is associated not only with the name of Sigmund Freud. He had colleagues and students who agreed with him in some ways and challenged his theory in others. As part of this series of books, you will be separately introduced to theories of personality by Adler and Jung, although they can also be included in the psychodynamic paradigm.

# SECTION 11. ESOTERIC ESSAY

## ANTHROPOMORPHIC IDEA OF THE HIGHER FORCES

Have you ever wondered how an esotericist differs from a representative of any particular traditional religion? I think that the main difference is that the esotericist explores the subtle worlds himself. He interprets them as he considers correct, and is sure that there can be no canon or dogma on this issue. The way we see such high and abstract concepts as God, Destiny or Mission is not as frozen monoliths but as a long road along which our ideas undergo constant transformation. The esotericist is a rebel in this respect. Until he is convinced himself, he is unlikely to take on faith in something that someone outside himself has told him about, except perhaps at the very beginning of his esoteric path. Even in such classical relationships as the guru and his disciple (if we are dealing with a real guru) the disciple is guided along the path, but he is never told what he must find at the end of this long road.

It is simply impossible to engage in any esoteric practice and not question such things as the structure of the Universe. But you must admit that our clients think much less about this than we do. A client who lives in the "real world" and only occasionally comes to mystical consultations, as a rule, has a complete concoction in his head regarding questions about God, Fate, Karma or Mission. The danger arises when, at the time of the consultation, the practitioner and their client consider these ideas very differently. If these world-view differences are not taken into account, we can cause serious harm to the client by careless interpretation.

The average client, who lives a normal life and only occasionally seeks counselling, usually has an anthropomorphic idea of Higher Forces. They see God as a masculine superbeing. Fate is more often represented as a woman, which originates from the mythology of various peoples, in which it is usually the goddesses who personify fate, and not the gods. Different languages assign different genders to death, and this influences how the figure of Death is imagined. However, why is it important for us to understand and take this into account?

The anthropomorphism of Higher Forces is expressed in our clients through the concepts of transference and countertransference. The Higher Forces are the parental figures in the unconscious of our clients; if a person had a punishing father or a cold and indifferent mother, then he will see God as punishing, and Fate as cold and indifferent. Some psychoanalysts, speaking on this subject, always mention the earliest periods of human mental development—as a rule, the preverbal infantile stage—when the degree of abstraction of everything is at its highest. Then, God is reduced to the concept of a good or bad mother's breast, on which the baby is completely dependent. It is good if the baby can feed and receive pleasure from the breast when they want to. But the breast can also violate this relationship with untimely meals, leaving the infant hungry, unhappy and feeling that he will not survive.

You can laugh, but from the point of view of the psychodynamic paradigm, such a theory makes a lot of sense. We are discussing this topic here because, for our client, we are representatives, deputies or heralds of those same anthropomorphic Higher Forces. Many authors in the same esoteric environment write that no matter how hard we try, the client hears our words differently from how he hears all other people. We broadcast mystical information that comes from a source about which the client has a very vague idea. Even if we do not attach any importance to this at all, the client may hear in our words punishment when we simply voice some criticism, a sentence when we simply talk about a variant future, or conversely, a mission while we are just talking about some stable feature of their character.

Such abstract questions are rarely discussed in consultations, but the tarot reader should consider in advance how his interpretations may sound. Of course, we cannot guarantee 100 percent how the client will perceive our words, and sometimes it is even useful to ask what they heard. Very often, one gets surprised by how what they've said is refracted in the mind of the client.

There are very benevolent phrases that can break down the negative transference of clients onto anthropomorphic Higher Forces. For example, I like to say the following: "Space does not need us to suffer. He needs us to develop." When the client hears this phrase, they begin to smile, as they understand that I myself do not consider the Higher Forces as prosecutors, and therefore, my words should not be heard as a sentence.

In our esoteric development, we do not immediately come to such a world view ourselves. It's just that the esotericist, in the course of training and independent searches, is gradually freed from such an anthropomorphic vision and begins to see God as a faceless Absolute, and the Higher Forces, rather, as neutral, but more positive and loving. But it is difficult to come to such a vision right away. Not that you need to talk about it to the client in the form of a metaphysical lecture about the structure of the Universe. But sometimes, in the course of communicating with you, the client receives a unique experience that turns their whole life upside down. Try to talk to the client sometime about a "karmic relationship". I am sure that you will hear a completely distorted explanation in the spirit of crime and punishment. For many clients, the real revelation is the information that karma can be positive, not just negative.

I have often had cases when a client has unwittingly become traumatised by such esoteric concepts, normally through reading something on the internet. I had a client who suffered for years from the fact that her daughter had Lilith (the Black Moon) in the horoscope in the eighth house, and she had read somewhere, or someone had told her, that this is a sure sign that in her daughter's life there will be early loss of the mother. You can imagine how anxious she was, overwhelmed all this time. It's good that she asked me about it herself. But such ideas firmly settle in the mind of the client only when the subtle world is seen as dangerous, and the Higher Forces are formidable and punishing.

You cannot penetrate the minds of your new clients and understand in advance through which world-view filter they perceive card interpretations. This can only be clarified if the client cooperates. If they are given the right to speak at consultations, if they understand that they will not be evaluated from the point of view of norm and pathology, or virtue and sin, they often begin to talk about things that concern not one specific situation in their life, but global existential issues. The client is usually very curious; they are just embarrassed to ask.

By the way, many clients are sure that a tarot reader, so wise and initiated into secrets, is forbidden to talk about these topics with him, such a stupid and secular little man. He does not even know how much such information has already been published. Sometimes it is helpful to recommend a book that you consider thorough on a given subject.

The client may not realise exactly what they're allowed to ask about at a consultation. Emotions—yes, events—yes, the future—yes, questions about how this world works from the point of view of esoteric philosophies—also yes! This is often very important for the client. It's like how doctors take informed consent for surgery from their patients. And the point is not at all a disclaimer of responsibility, but an ethical respect for the client's right to know what he is involved in.

# SECTION 12. PROBLEMS OF THE TAROT COMMUNITY

## Criteria for Competent Tarot Consultation

This is an extremely difficult topic. If we were not esotericists but, say, traditional doctors or teachers, it would be an easier question to answer. But how do you formulate the criteria for competent work in a field where there is no single standard?

In fact, there is a completely transparent and unambiguous answer to this question, but I am afraid that it will greatly disappoint many: "Competent tarot consultation is the completion of the contract with the client." Disappointment arises from the fact that each practitioner has their own contract—and no one except you can tell you exactly what it should contain. However, let's speculate on this topic, and then, perhaps, the situation will become somewhat clearer.

Let's start with an absolutely blasphemous question. "What exactly are you selling?" I am sure that many tarologists have never even asked themselves such a question, but knowing the answer will help to make sure you and your clients are on the same page. The client comes to you with some expectations, and the true indicator of a competent consultation is the client's satisfaction after the consultation. Knowing exactly what service you offer, and making this clear to the client, will help to ensure their satisfaction.

I periodically refer to research I have done with other tarot readers. Usually, when describing a competent consultation, they mention two components. First, the client must receive information, usually of a predictive or clairvoyant nature. In other words, you must say something about the client's past or present that you cannot know, but the client can confirm, or, you must give a prediction that must certainly come true. Secondly, the psycho-emotional state of the client should improve after the consultation. It is interesting that even those tarologists who oppose the integration of tarot and psychology write about this. It turns out that the tarologist performs two functions: he is clairvoyant and he is a psychologist.

"What exactly are you selling?" I will repeat this question, as the answer dictates the format and style of your work. If you are selling the future, then you need to get your interpretations into the client's event stream as accurately as possible. I am sure that tarot cards are capable of this, otherwise the system would not have lived and been developed for so long. It is curious, though, that there are no tarologists who can do this with absolute accuracy. According to my observations, they are quite often successful, but not always. And it is not yet possible to understand what exactly this accuracy depends on.

Of course, it is possible to take a dominant approach to consulting and sentence our clients to the future that falls in the cards. There are practitioners who do this. But it's impossible to control the client's reaction. Yes, there are suggestible clients, and they can be led to start the process of a self-fulfilling prophecy. Then the predicted future happens not because you guessed it, but because you voiced it dominantly. And if the client has an anthropomorphic vision of Higher Forces, they will obediently fulfil the voiced prophecy, make a substitution in their consciousness and say that you are a prophet.

I must admit that I know very few colleagues who work this way. In the same study, colleagues noted that they considered a dominant work style to be one of the worst qualities a tarot reader could have. It turns out that if a practitioner chooses this style of work, they run the risk of being left without peer support, or even being completely rejected by the professional community and left alone. Therefore, the future is dangerous to sell.

Most tarologists compromise and say that they are selling a variant future. By saying this, they mean the following: there is no fixed future, but there are options for it, which depend on the real client and their choices in the here and now. As soon as the client changes in the present, their future will change. "So, these tarologists are relieving themselves of responsibility for unfulfilled predictions," you say. But maybe that's just the way it is with the future. Maybe the future is really variant, and then the whole focus of the consultation is completely shifted. It becomes important for you not to give an accurate prediction of the future, but to help the client make a choice in such a way that they are satisfied with the future that will be brought about.

The question is whether the client understands this. For this reason, preliminary instruction is needed. If the client agrees that the tarot reader does not necessarily need to provide a sparkling and perfect prediction, but that their role is to make it easier for the client to make a decision by voicing all the alternatives, then everything becomes much clearer. By this definition, a competent tarot consultation is one that works this way, helping the client get out of an impasse of development. That is, the situation should become easier and more understandable for the client. Yes, this can happen without intentional psychological work, and I think that opponents of the integration of tarot and psychology often fall back on this fact.

However, that's not the only requirement for a successful consultation. I agree with everything described above. But if that was all there was to it, then there would be no point in this series of books. Clients definitely want something else but do not say it because, perhaps, they are not aware themselves. They want to experience some interaction that they cannot get in their ordinary lives. But what can we do that family, friends or colleagues, who certainly know the client much better than us, cannot do? Maybe, though, these people are the problem, and the client needs a clear mirror in which they can be reflected.

Here we really get very close to the format of psychotherapy. The fundamental rule regarding the relationship between a therapist and client is that it can only be a professional relationship. They are not friends, not colleagues, not family. The client buys the therapist's time, during which they receive an unbiased reflection of themselves by a person who is not only a specialist in mental processes and knows where to look, but who definitely will not bring their own psychological material into it. This is a very valuable experience that is absolutely impossible to get anywhere except in psychotherapy.

It is also impossible to get it in tarot, in my opinion. Everything depends on the format of work. Therapy is a long-term process, and the results are obtained, among other reasons, because it takes a long time and takes place regularly. The therapist has plenty of time to gain the client's trust, work with their resistance, test their hypotheses, listen to themselves and understand what is changing in the countertransference, and simply accompany the client through the changes that come slowly. In tarot we deal most often with a single visit. What can we do in such a short amount of time?

We are definitely not psychotherapists, and we do not conduct psychotherapy with a client. I really hope that in the course of reading these books you will be able to firmly grasp this. Then why do we need all these psychological tools? Well, today I have a tentative answer to this question, though I cannot say for sure it will not change in the future.

You may be surprised if I tell you the following: I have completed full psychotherapeutic training and have many colleagues in this field, more than half of whom have visited me for tarot consultations. What's happening? Why do they come? Am I selling them the future? Or are they satisfied with the variant future that we are looking at? They know better than anyone else where to go for psychotherapy. They themselves say that even if they're ready to try tarot, they're only interested in having me as their tarologist. And not because I am such a cool tarologist, but because I am the only tarologist they know who understands psychotherapy. I am safe for them. And again, the question: "What exactly do we sell?"

I've thought a lot about this, and have come to the following conclusion: "We're selling an hour of concentrated time." I'll explain. The fact is that tarot cards have a very interesting effect. While working with them, the very perception of time changes. The client sees a symbolic picture in front of them in which their past, present and future converge. Time, usually stretched in a straight line, is concentrated here, and a certain effect of timelessness appears. This is an absolutely transpersonal experience that cannot be obtained in a psychotherapist's office.

But that's not all. When a client asks about their loved ones (if, of course, the tarot reader works with such questions), in one picture a panorama unfolds not only of their inner world but also the world of the one they've asked about. The subject-object boundary between them and another person becomes thinner, in a timeless picture (past, present and future, all at once). Through tarot, this experience can be obtained in a safe, psychological format. But what is the value of this experience?

If you refer to the works of famous mystics, for example, Jiddu Krishnamurti, you will find that in this state the mind stops, and you enter a slightly altered state of consciousness, in which there is less anxiety. All anxiety comes from the concept of the future. No future; no anxiety. There is no clear boundary between me and the other; there is also no anxiety. It's not that we bring our clients to a similar mystical state during tarot consultations. Of course not. This can come only in the course of regular long-term meditations, raja yoga. But for a moment, we bring the client a little closer to this state. This causes an inner transformation. It's like we're rebooting the client's mind computer, which has begun to glitch. No, we didn't clean the viruses from its hard drive—that is exactly what a psychotherapist will do. But for a moment we give a person an experience that removes those basic elements of suffering that are inherent in everyone: the illusion of psychological time and separation from others. This significantly reduces the existential anxiety of the client, giving them the resources to sort out their problem.

You can ask me: "And this is exactly what you sell at tarot consultations?" No, I'm not selling this. It is also impossible to guarantee the client, as in the case of Fred in the earlier vignette. If the client doesn't want it, it's impossible to arrange it. I am selling a perspective on the client's life in which these experiences can occur. I suggest that the client looks at their situation in this way. But what I absolutely guarantee is a psychologically safe space for such an immersion. Of course, the client in the contract understands this somewhat differently. For them, it sounds simpler: "I want to see how my life is seen from an esoteric perspective, and I want to do this with a reliable, psychologically safe guide."

I think that everyone has their own criteria for a competent tarot consultation. I don't really care much about whether my predictions come true. To be honest, after the consultation, I don't remember anything that I predicted. What is important is that I see changes in a person before and after the consultation itself. If I see a change in their emotional state, a decrease in anxiety, the acquisition of new meanings for their life and situation, and they feel more active and confident, understood and supported, then I have worked well.

It doesn't always work out. There are clients or cases where I am powerless. The case of Fred is just one such example. But such cases do not affect my professional self-esteem.

I also value honest and trusting relationships with my clients. I'm glad when they come back, even if I don't even remember them. I am pleased not when they say that all my predictions came true, but when they note how much easier things have become for them after the last consultation, with what pleasure and interest they later listened to the recording of the consultation, and how accurately we managed to discern their condition and problems.

# PART TWO

# SECTION 1. ZODIAC

## King of Wands – Leo

### *Upright Position*

Probably the most important difference between the Queen and King of Wands is the nature of the energy flow that they transmit. In the first case, we talked about a powerful impulse or energy release. With the Queen of Wands, energy never flows smoothly. It is explosive, and the impulse is so powerful that it disables the ability to think clearly. The King of Wands has an energy flow no less powerful, but it is absolutely even and stable. If the Queen is a geyser, then the King is a wide, full-flowing river. And since the energy flow takes the form of a particular idea, it becomes clear how this idea manifests itself in the life of a particular person. If the Queen of Wands is constantly in need of a lofty idea that she can bring to the world like a prophet, doing it sacrificially, forgetting about her personality, then the King of Wands can be called the viceroy of such an idea on Earth. He guards it, he rules it, and in the end he comes to completely personify it.

This difference is, in fact, huge. The Queen of Wands transmits an idea, forgetting about herself. And the King of Wands translates himself through an idea. He does this consciously, and as he does so, it is very important to him how he looks, how others react to him, and how high his status is.

Like any character of this suit, the King of Wands is a natural leader. He initially has much more energy and strength than those around him. He has such large reserves that he can share them with others, give others gifts, patronise them and lead them. Fire represents honesty and nobility. Usually, no one doubts the rights of such a king to the throne. He is really very strong and noticeable, and, of course, he knows this very well.

In general, the King of Wands, from birth, considers himself better than others. This is a natural narcissism, a feeling of being chosen which cannot be removed in any way—and it is not necessary to because it is partly true. Indeed, he was given more than others, but it is important to remember that he is only the viceroy of the idea and not its owner. The idea will only energise him as long as he correctly transmits it. As soon as he distorts the idea or believes that without him there would be no idea at all, the energy flow becomes thinner, and he loses his glow and leadership charm.

The King of Wands is quite noble, and he is completely devoid of sadism. If a conflict occurs, then he first lets out a menacing growl, like a lion, marking the boundaries of his power and reminding everyone of who is in charge. If the opponent does not let up and continues to attack, then only one powerful blow will follow, which knocks the person down. But the King of Wands will never chase down a fleeing enemy and finish him off, or revel in his pain and suffering. This is generally not characteristic of the figures of the suit of Wands.

If the Queen of Wands has always needed enthusiasm and inspiration to keep her energy levels high, the King of Wands uses a different fuel. Positioning himself as the viceroy of the idea, it is very important for him to receive admiration for it. He's an actor on stage who wants applause. Such people are indeed somewhat theatrical and even pretentious, but they can be forgiven for this, since they really do cause people to admire them. The problem is that King of Wands is dependent on praise, dependent on the positive impression that he causes in others. He must be liked, he must be loved, otherwise he will suffer greatly from the lack of positive feedback. Such people really need to be praised a little more than average. This is very important to them, even though they look powerful and regal.

Let's look at an example. Take parenthood as a noble idea. In the case of King of Wands, we will get a stable, caring and very resourceful parent. He will invest responsibly in this role, but it is very important for him to be noticed and appreciated for it. His children should be grateful and proud of him, and others should see him as the parent of the year. The Queen of Wands, by the way, would not become a parent or take care of someone herself, if this was her idea. She only preaches the idea, so, she would inspire everyone to worthy parenthood, and say how noble and important it is, but she herself would not do it.

The King of Wands is a real king in the truest sense of the word. If he is in his place, does everything right and does not abuse his power and strength, he begins to glow. Surrounding people, seeing this glow, cannot but experience admiration. You can observe this effect every time someone is in their correct place. Life goes so smoothly, beautifully and powerfully that Universal order and harmony begin to emerge behind them. At such moments, such a person rises somewhat above others. He is on the stage, and the rest become his spectators. This is such a beautiful performance, there is so much glory in it, that it never occurs to anyone that they could take the place of such an artist, ousting him from the stage. Instead, it seems that this play, the scenery, and the whole theatre were made specifically for him. One has only to replace him with someone else, and everything begins to lose its meaning.

### *Reversed Position*

The main problem with the reversed King of Wands is an over-inflated ego. At some point, he forgets that the idea he embodies is not himself. The problem is exactly the same as that of the reversed Queen of Wands, who, without her energy flow, has a very poor idea of who she is. Her inner core is extremely weak. The reversed King of Wands also has no other stable identity without his idea. That is why he is so fiercely protective of it. If we look at the parenting example again, the reversed King of Wands will simply prevent his child from separating from him when she reaches adulthood. Without the parenting role, there is no reversed King of Wands. It will also be hard for him to live through his child's developmental crises, as it threatens the stability of the parental image. And if, God forbid, we are talking about modern family models—for example, a child-free family—then the reversed King of Wands faces a real threat, as an idea that is completely contrary to his values appears and gains supporters.

The Queen of Wands is able to change her idea and switch to something new. Yes, it costs her a period of depression and emptiness, but then the flow returns with renewed vigour, and everything is fine. The reversed King of Wands is firmly attached to his idea. He is not able to change the flow, which makes him vulnerable. Of course, in order to maintain his royal status, his retinue and luminosity, he invests not in the idea that he has transmitted and which nourished him, but in the external surroundings, in the false facade of his greatness.

It is very important for the reversed King of Wands to look good and broadcast an image of success. He begins to spend a colossal amount on this, turning into a classic malignant narcissist. Outside, we see luxury, splendour, a constant emphasis on pleasure, but inside such a person is completely empty. The people surrounding him are used only for the sake of exalting him with praise and admiration. They turn into a function of maintaining this false greatness.

The idea has long since abandoned the reversed King of Wands. It has found itself a new viceroy, more flexible, better suited to its essence. But the reversed King of Wands does not even think about leaving his throne. He clings to it with all his might. Instead of spending his rich resources on guarding and protecting the people around him, who admire him and his idea, he spends this energy solely on maintaining his own power.

Here it is, the formula of classic dictatorship. A true king does not need to suppress his followers. He is loved, respected; no one doubts his right to a leadership position. And such a king simply does what he must: provide his subjects with the level of life, comfort and security that his idea requires. But the reversed King of Wands, somewhere in the depths of his soul, feels that he has become an impostor. Yes, he was once the rightful leader, but now he is steadily losing followers. He is no longer admired; he is not idolised. And the easiest solution is to make them love him. The reversed King of Wands has enough strength for this. He will brutally suppress any dissent and quash any disagreement with his right to power.

There is one more detail that is common to all characters of the suit of Wands. It's the lack of subtlety. The power of the stream that they transmit leaves no opportunity to slow down or pay attention to details. Wands is a rather rough suit. Sometimes, the King of Wands' rudeness is forgivable because this is not a place for subtlety. The nobility of the flow forgives being tactless. In a reversed form, though, this rudeness is obvious and absolutely inappropriate, since it no longer serves the idea, but only the egoism of its bearer.

This makes the suit of Wands not particularly smart or cunning. Everything is about strength. But if there is not enough strength, which happens when the flow changes or when it is crushed, then for the sake of energy, the figures of the suit of Wands become ready for anything. They are energy addicts experiencing the strongest withdrawal.

In the case of the reversed King of Wands, flattery becomes a drug. It is important to note that this is no longer sincere admiration or an honest recognition of greatness, but false flattery that skilled manipulators use to get what they need from him. He will always be surrounded by such flatterers and leeches. They will support his ego every day and tell him how great, irreplaceable and strong he is. And the reversed King of Wands will pay them generously, as they are part of his luxurious entourage. Without them, the truth will become obvious to everyone: he is a naked king, who has long lost his crown and his chosen position. But the realisation of this is tantamount to destruction, since inside he is completely empty. Therefore, the reversed King of Wands will unconsciously believe any flattery, even the most mediocre, although it will be obvious to everyone around him that he is simply being manipulated.

# SECTION 2. VIGNETTE

## EMPRESS TAKES OFF HER CROWN, CHAPTER 3

"Maybe it will still work out today."

Emma did not quite understand whether the client on the other end of the phone was making a request or stating a fact. She paced nervously around her apartment, trying to figure out her schedule for the day. It was one of those days when she had to do a dozen things at the same time, and as luck would have it, that was when all the clients needed to see her for a consultation.

"Please understand," said Emma. "Tomorrow, definitely, with pleasure. Today I just have nowhere to put you on the schedule."

"I have very urgent questions regarding work. Decisions must be made today; tomorrow it will be too late," the client insisted.

"If so, if you want, I can recommend my colleague to you. She is free today. I think she will definitely accept you."

"No, I would like to see you." The client did not calm down. "You were recommended to me. I only want to see you—no one else. I can pay twice as much for the inconvenience."

Emma was conflicted. She did not normally do such things and felt extremely uncomfortable. There was a desperate struggle inside her: take the client or refuse him. It wasn't about the money at all. She was hooked by knowing that someone so positively recommended her. It was like she'd just beaten other tarologists in a prestigious competition.

"You don't need twice as much," Emma said. "Let's do it. I will have an hour available today from five to six. This is my only free time. But at six, we'll have to finish. It's four thirty p.m., can you make it?"

"Yes, I can!" the client agreed.

Emma put the phone down and exhaled. *Work questions*. It sometimes happens that a decision needs to be made urgently. She remembered this well from her career in the office. Any serious job very quickly acquires a tendency to become overtime. Success doesn't come on schedule; it has to be caught. But it was always so stressful! Emma wasn't exactly mad at the client right now, it's just that the day wasn't working out how she'd planned in the morning; everything was falling out of her hands.

Tom, whom she had run into in an elevator about three months ago, turned out to be married. The next day, he'd invited her to his place to get acquainted. His wife, Liz, turned out to be a sweet and pleasant woman. Tom and Liz fit together amazingly, like two pieces of clothing from one set. Friendly relations between the three began quickly and naturally. They'd visited each other several times since, to talk or borrow things from each other. Emma really liked Liz. They were about the same age. Liz worked at a school as an English language and literature teacher with older children. Perhaps it was an interest in books that had brought her and Tom together.

Emma really liked her new friends. It was always very easy and fun with them, and also very convenient, since all she had to do was leave the apartment and walk along a small corridor to see them.

After some time, Emma, not without difficulty, had confessed to her new friends about her occupation. They weren't surprised at all.

"We saw what kind of books you have on the shelves," they'd answered in unison.

It seemed that they'd been waiting for her to tell them about it, so they hadn't asked questions. And then they asked for some time, with childish curiosity, in a good way, since they were obviously very interested. Emma had felt much better after this conversation like a stone had fallen from her soul. She did not hear any condemnation or even unhealthy curiosity and an immediate request to lay out cards for them.

Later, Liz came to her for a reading but never abused her status as a neighbour or friend. After working with her, Emma realised that Liz and Tom were just the kind of people who don't really need cards, since everything in their lives was more or less in order. They supported each other very well, and generally preferred more secular ways of solving problems, although they did not deride the tarot method at all.

Liz was far more worried about something else: why didn't Emma have a boyfriend? This was no senile moaning about how Emma was still single. Liz, rather, was perplexed, and her care seemed sisterly. She and Tom were a very strong couple, and she simply did not understand how it was possible to live alone. She had not pressed, seeing that Emma was embarrassed to talk about this subject. But their friendship had developed quickly, and one day, Liz suggested that she should meet John, a guy from her work. A blind date. Emma hadn't felt that uncomfortable in a long time. She'd refused a dinner, but went for coffee with this John that morning.

She'd thought that John would also be a teacher of literature or history, but he'd turned out to be a school gym teacher. Conversation with him hadn't gone well. Emma felt absolutely terrible after that morning coffee. The worst thing was that she had arranged with Tom and Liz that she would go to theirs for a glass of wine at six, this evening, since on Thursdays they often gathered for a friendly chat. Well, they were definitely going to ask how everything went. Emma was sure that Liz had already told Tom everything; they seemed to have no secrets from each other at all. Not that Emma particularly cared. It wasn't a date, just morning coffee. Liz had wanted Emma's expert opinion on John and why he'd been so unlucky in relationships. And Emma definitely had a lot of experience in dealing with people. If she didn't like John, then at least she could share what, in her opinion, was wrong with him. This had not been a date, but an expert assessment.

The doorbell interrupted Emma's thoughts. The client really had managed to get there in half an hour.

On the threshold stood a young man, about thirty-five years old, dressed in an expensive business suit. For a moment, Emma felt like she was at a prestigious business forum. Her hands even instinctively crawled up to straighten the collar of her blouse. The posture and position of the man's head, as well as the haughty look, suggested to Emma that in front of her was not an ordinary employee, but rather a manager. The man introduced himself as Brian and held out his hand for a handshake. Emma invited him into her study, where he sat down in a chair and immediately began:

"Thank you very much for agreeing to receive me promptly. I'm here on a recommendation from my colleagues, Pete and Jack. They spoke very positively about you. They said that you are doing miracles here. That's why I didn't want anyone else, you know? I only want a professional."

Emma felt a little strange. On the one hand, it was nice to be praised, and that other clients had recommended her. On the other hand, she did not remember when she'd performed any miracles. If that was the basis for their recommendation, then the clients most likely perceived her work differently from how she did. Moreover, she did not remember at all who they were—Pete and Jack. But that was not surprising. She'd learned to put a client out of her thoughts as soon as the door closed behind them. She felt that these clients had raised the bar higher than she wanted. Situations like this always made her feel a bit stressed. Clients very often perceived cards with much more reverence than she herself.

"I can't promise miracles, but I'll try my best," Emma replied. "What would you like to see?"

Brian nodded and continued. "I have a very important choice to make at my job. We are a large IT company, and I have always had people under me, and my superiors have always kept me in good standing. Now the company is taking on three new projects, which would involve relocation to other countries. I need to lead one of these projects and, accordingly, move to another country for three years. I was given the first choice. There are two more project managers who will get the other two options.

"I would like to make this choice correctly. I feel that my career depends on what I say to the founder tomorrow. Hence the urgency. I don't want to be wrong."

Emma sighed with relief. It was quite a common request for cards. She already knew how to deal with such a question.

"Could you list the countries in question for me?" she asked.

"Yes, sure. They're Germany, Poland and the USA."

Emma shuffled the deck and laid out a twelve-card pattern on the table. Each column of the spread corresponded to a given country in the order that the client had listed them. The rows represented three aspects of the situation. Emma already knew from experience that everyone who asks about work is actually interested in something different. One person cares about raising their status, someone else might be interested in money, while a third cares for the social component. The fourth row represented compatibility with the country and culture. This was usually of interest to all relocators, since not every cultural environment suits every individual.

The cards turned out like this:

| GERMANY | POLAND | USA |
|---|---|---|

"So, let's discuss in turn what we have got here," Emma began. "In terms of status and influence, Germany and the United States are the strongest. The difference is that in Germany your status will be more solid, and I would say positive. In the US, it looks like you will have power and influence, but there it seems like you will constantly have some fear that someone may claim your place. A sort of feeling of paranoia, when you can't quite rely on the people around you. They may obey you, but out of fear."

"And Poland?" Brian asked.

"In Poland, your role does not quite look like a leader. It's more like playing second fiddle. I would suggest that there will be another person who will stand above you, and you will have to obey him in many ways."

"That's your first miracle," said Brian admiringly. "I didn't tell you, but the founder, to whom I have to give an answer tomorrow, is going to Warsaw himself. If I went there, the project would be led by me, as it were, but at the same time, my boss would constantly stand behind my back. You are a magician!"

Emma blushed a little. She felt her enthusiasm and excitement rise in her. It's a tantalising feeling when you hit the target—you want to try again and again in order to consolidate that success and make sure it can't be attributed to chance or dumb luck.

She continued her interpretation.

"From the point of view of money, the United States still looks the best. The money is really big. It might not come to you right away; this is more about the potential of the project. But to be honest, something else bothers me. Though the money's good, other things don't come together smoothly. There is a constant turnover of people here. The feeling is that it will not be possible to recruit a stable team. And this may also mean that you yourself will be disappointed in this option, since something will be wrong with the country itself and life there."

"I don't like the States," Brian agreed. "Again, bingo! However, my personal preference is of no interest to anyone here at all. I just need to win this race, that's all."

Emma was glad to be right again. There was something very pleasant in the way the client, in front of her, reacted to her correct answers. Clients did not always give feedback, and then it could become especially difficult to work. There was something about Brian that gave Emma confidence in herself. She once had a boss in her office who'd often praised her. It was nice and made her try harder and harder. From somewhere, additional energy would appear which removed all her fatigue and doubts.

"Germany," Emma continued, "is also a good option. There will be good and stable money, as well as the opportunity to influence the distribution of resources yourself. What confuses me, though, is that there you seem to have trouble navigating among the employees. This card"—Emma pointed to the Eight of Swords—"says that you will seem to be blindfolded and your hands are tied. And the country itself is not quite suitable for you. It will be difficult to settle down there, as if you will feel like a stranger."

Brian looked amazed.

"I will definitely have to buy Pete and Jack a beer. No wonder they recommended you to me. I had my doubts, to be honest. You know, they could have set me up. But the fact is that in Germany there will be a completely foreign-language team. I won't know anyone there. But you say that the status there is high?"

"Yes," Emma confirmed. "Although, from the sum of everything that has fallen here, Poland looks the best. There may be less in terms of money, but it is somehow especially good in terms of people and the country itself. Something tells me you'll love it there. And relations with colleagues there are good—very good, even."

Brian smiled. "I'll explain what's going on here," he said. "It's that the founder is bringing most of our current office to Warsaw with him. I more or less know everyone who will go there. Not that they are nice people, just acquaintances. You're right, I won't have to get to know them."

Emma felt like she had won the lottery. She was not always able to work so clearly and accurately. And this despite the fact that the client had given her almost no clues. The stars must have aligned today.

Emma leaned back in her chair, satisfied with her work. Now she no longer regretted taking this client, despite such a busy day.

"Yes. So, Poland?" she asked.

Brian looked at her in surprise. His gaze changed, became a little colder, and his head again raised itself somewhat arrogantly.

"Why Poland?" he wondered. "It'll be the States, of course."

Emma was a little confused. She'd been sure that the client would choose Poland.

"Wait," she said. "Do I understand correctly that you're choosing the States because there is the biggest money there and good status? You just said that you don't particularly like the country."

"I don't," Brian agreed. "But I'm ready to be patient. I don't want to work under the founder anymore. More precisely, I would still be under him—this is his business, after all. But I don't want him breathing down my neck."

Emma felt strange. She'd started off so well, but now it was like something has happened to her sensitivity. She definitely did not like the option with the States. On the other hand, she understood that Brian would decide for himself. All she could do was accurately convey what the cards showed. No need to impose on him what she liked herself. But something kept her from calming down. There was a feeling that, just a minute, ago a huge ball of light and warmth had been growing in her chest, but it had suddenly burst, burning everything inside with some kind of feeling that Emma still did not understand.

"Will you go alone, or with your wife?" she asked.

"I'm not married," the client snapped. "And what does that have to do with it?"

"I just thought," Emma replied, "that moving to a foreign country for three years is not an easy task. If you are in a relationship, then for a couple this can be an intolerable test. Usually, people solve such serious issues together. I just thought that if this is an important aspect, then Poland looks better because socially you look like a strong and reliable couple there. While in the United States, there is a breakdown and departure. However, that could be to do with your relationship with the founder. Do you need to check the topic of your relationships?"

Brian looked a little confused. It was clear he was not particularly comfortable answering this question. His very image seemed to flicker. At first, a polished and successful alpha sat in front of Emma, a winner and a triumph, but the man lost all his brilliance, became dull and seemed like a very frightened and insecure boy.

Emma didn't rush him. He sat for a while in silence, as if considering options and deciding on something.

"I have a girlfriend, actually," he said. "But this decision is not for her to make. As I decide, so it will be. But what if I chose Poland, would she go with me?"

"Perhaps she would," said Emma. "Do you want us to add a row of cards in order to understand how the whole situation will look like if we include her?"

Brian nodded. And Emma added three more cards at the bottom of the spread.

She was pleased with what the cards showed, as they fully confirmed her hypothesis. Surely, the Five of Pentacles was confirming the fact that Brian's girlfriend would go to Germany for him, but this would only burden the whole situation. It was a card of a painful and dependent union. Most likely, in Germany, she would cling to Brian and have no independence. She would not go to the USA at all, as the Hermit frankly said. Brian would go there alone, and that would be the end of the relationship. But in Poland, at least she would find friends and company. It was the most emotionally acceptable option.

"Does she work?" Emma asked Brian.

"She's doing something for charity." Brian snorted contemptuously. "I never really got into it."

"I mean, only in Poland she could continue her activities. I think that she would not dare to go to the States. And in Germany, she looks completely dependent on you. Only in Poland—"

"She is completely dependent on me." Her client interrupted irritably. "I repeat once again, this is not her decision, but exclusively mine."

He was definitely getting angry, and Emma suddenly felt very uncomfortable with this client. It was as if something had happened to make her feel small and incompetent and stupid. She understood what this feeling was that was burning her from the inside. It was a shame she knew too well. But where had she gone wrong? What had she said? After all, she herself believed—no, she was absolutely sure of what she'd said a minute ago: when it comes to such issues as moving to another country, a couple must decide together. But now it felt simply unbearable for her to voice this opinion again.

She sensed that there was indeed something wrong with how she was looking at the question. What the hell was she doing here anyway?

Emma nodded and obediently said, "Of course. You decide."

Brian sat opposite in silence, as if he expected something more from her. But she didn't know what to do. She usually asked clients if they had any more questions, but now this simple trick for some reason did not occur to her. Why had she even talked about the topic of relationships? After all, the client had not asked about it. It was her who'd begun to impose on him an angle that was not voiced in the request. She'd broken her own rules. And she also remembered how at the tarot school, the teacher had repeated especially clearly and many times: "Do not scratch where it doesn't itch!", meaning that never, under any circumstances, should a tarot practitioner answer questions that haven't been asked.

This had all become somehow completely unbearable. Why did she go there? Had she wanted to show off? Ugh!

But still, Emma gathered herself and was able to continue:

"Is there anything else you would like to ask?" she said.

Brian, who had gone somewhere in his thoughts, suddenly surfaced.

"Anything else?" he asked. "What else do they usually ask?"

"Well, I don't know," said Emma. She would very much like him to ask one more question so she could rehabilitate herself. "They ask about relationships, about hobbies, about money, friends, trips. Although your question was so voluminous that—"

"Yes." Brian simply nodded. "I think that's all." He glanced around the room, peering slowly at the surrounding objects, and then added, "Perhaps this just isn't for me."

He stood up and shook Emma's hand. Without another word, he walked towards the exit. At the door he stopped, suddenly remembering that he had not paid. He took out his wallet and put the required amount on the shelf by the door. Then, he simply left the apartment.

Emma remained standing in the corridor. The whole consultation had lasted, at most, fifteen minutes, although she'd allowed an hour for it. That would've been great! Even before Brian arrived, Emma had had doubts about taking on an extra client today. He had not fit into her plans. But now she had completely forgotten about what she'd had planned. She really hadn't wanted Brian to leave so quickly. She hadn't yet had time to really start working, and now she felt like a novice musician who'd come to a famous producer for an audition, only to be cut off literally on the second note with the phrase: "Thank you, that's enough! We will contact you."

# SECTION 3. CHARACTEROLOGY

## The Narcissistic Character

One interesting thing about psychological terms is that they quite often fall into common usage, and then they do not quite have the same meaning that professionals put into them. "Narcissism", if we talk about it in a purely psychological way, is far from necessarily bad. If a person is proud of their real achievements, knows how to beautifully demonstrate their talents and, in some situations, deliberately behaves in such a way as to gain the admiration and recognition of others, there is absolutely nothing wrong with that. Any person in childhood necessarily goes through a narcissistic period, which is extremely important for the formation of positive and stable self-esteem. This is healthy narcissism. But unfortunately, there is also a malignant form, which we will discuss in this section.

Each epoch and every civilisation has accentuated certain traits in people, making one character radical, or another the leading one. In the modern Western world, narcissism has become an epidemic. Being focused on success, achievement and positive feedback is considered the norm today. In psychological literature, one can come across the remark that the narcissistic character today has burst far ahead and replaced the histrionic character that once dominated Freud's time, which we will consider in the third part of this book. In other words, it has become simply impossible to live in modern society and not encounter narcissism.

## Childhood

We have already said several times that all people need reflection. This is how our psyche works. We begin to understand who we are based on the way that people around us react to us. This is true throughout the entirety of a person's life, but is especially important in childhood, when the child's personality is being formed. To understand who he is, a child must see himself reflected competently and clearly by the adults involved in his upbringing.

What will happen if the child's parents, for various reasons, constantly praise and encourage him when he does something that they like, and frustrate and punish the child when he does something that he likes himself? This is just one of the prerequisites for the child to begin to intensively develop in himself the narcissistic radical of character. The life of many modern children is scheduled literally by the minute. There are numerous courses, sports and tutors, which the child does not always attend because he himself has chosen to do so. It's just that the child's parents are preparing him for a successful adult life, so they initially form his schedule so that he constantly improves and achieves results. However, to be honest, one has to admit one sad fact: such children often do not work for their own future success, but to satisfy the desires of their parents.

If a mother was not sent to a ballet school as a child, since there was no such opportunity, then she will definitely make her child a prima ballerina. If Dad was kicked out of the hockey team for poor results as a child, then his son will certainly achieve significant results and medals in hockey. The bar of success and achievement in such families usually rises so high that even an adult would be afraid of such a difficult task. Here it is placed in front of a still-fragile child, but the result is demanded from him with the same severity and ruthlessness.

It is impossible to talk about narcissism without mentioning such a complex feeling as shame. The parents of the future narcissist are themselves filled with toxic shame. Shame, at its core, has a tricky setup. It is generally accepted that a person is ashamed when they feel they are morally bad. I think that this is not entirely true. A person feels shame when they do not know who they are and when they do not have the experience of being reflected in a similar situation. The parents of a narcissist have never experienced real success and achievement themselves. Therefore, they cannot talk about this subject without shame because they simply do not understand what it is like. By virtue of their age and missed opportunities, it is already too late for them to conquer the heights of success. This mission is now assigned to the child. He was supposed to live his own life. Now he lives to please his parents.

How is the child to survive if faced with the task of living not his own, but someone else's life? He needs to develop his personality, but no one thinks to reflect him in the present with his desires. Therefore, the child is forced to form what, in psychology, is commonly called a False Self. This is a structure with a huge shining facade, designed to make a grand impression on the people around, but inside such a "building" there are only bare, reinforced concrete walls. It is very difficult to live inside such a structure, but (most importantly), in no case should other people be allowed inside; they must be kept outside to admire the facade. It would be very embarrassing if they went inside and saw how pathetic and miserable everything looked.

Such a kid in childhood is constantly criticised and compared with someone else. Whatever the child does, Johnny, the boy next door, does it better, and classmate Mary will always arouse more admiration in his parents than he does. The child has to try even harder, as it is unfair. He is his parents' son, not Johnny or Mary. But this eternal criticism, the fear of losing in comparison with others, becomes tightly built into the structure of the child's personality. He begins to compete and compete in all areas and then transfers this quality into adulthood.

Although the following phrase is never said verbatim to the child, this is exactly the message that he hears from his parents all the time: "I will only love you if you are the way I want you to be." Of course, the result of such a message will be permanently weak self-esteem and an extreme dependence on one's own achievements and results. After all, every child wants to be loved.

## Adulthood

As we said at the beginning of this section, narcissism is very widely supported in society today. It is fashionable to be successful, noticeable and popular. Many people invest a lot of effort in promoting themselves, in creating the right image. And if this is a working environment, then there is an opportunity to achieve good results. Narcissists can indeed be quite successful in their work, making big money and enjoying wide influence. The only problem is that it is difficult for them to stop and enjoy it.

The narcissist is always insatiable inside. All the admiration and praise he receives goes into a black hole. The self-esteem of a narcissist is like a leaky vessel that simply cannot be filled. There is nothing surprising here, since the narcissist has never satisfied his own needs in his life. He has always worked for someone else's needs. Therefore, it is very difficult for him to appropriate the results. He needs constant admiration and confirmation of his success, since he himself does not believe in it, and he is afraid of exposure and criticism. It is much more difficult to please society than a parent, since society is many-faced and poorly understood. Tension increases exponentially in adulthood.

Narcissists are very difficult when in contact with other people. They act like they're on the catwalk and the cameras are constantly pointing at them. They are beautiful marble statues that work only to receive admiration. They can't give you anything in return. Narcissists are cold and arrogant, even if they manage to attract the attention they're after. If you came to admire them, then everything is in order. But if you expect the same admiration from them, or even a little attention, you will simply get nothing. The narcissist perceives you as a mirror for self-admiration. You are not seen as a separate person with your own needs and feelings. You are just a function that you must perform properly. The narcissist does exactly the same thing to you that his parents did to him as a child: he refuses to see your individuality but uses you to expand his own importance.

Even if in their career they manage to stay in contact, then in the romantic sphere, narcissists are not capable of creating fully fledged and happy unions. Energy flows only in one direction. The partner is perceived either as a function or as a convenient accessory, which only serves to reinforce and improve the luxurious image of its owner. In a relationship with a narcissist, it is extremely cold and lonely. You can forget about your needs. You have to spend all your strength on servicing not even the narcissist himself, but his false facade, which he has created all his life.

Narcissists fail to build, among other things, warm long-term relationships because it is difficult for them to experience and express two ordinary human feelings: guilt and gratitude. This means that they do not know how to apologise and thank when it is necessary; they do not know how to say "sorry" and "thank you". These two simple words, without which relationships cannot be built, are very dangerous for narcissists. They hint at their imperfection and humanity, which can cause their facade to crumble. To admit that you are guilty of something means to doubt your own infallibility. To thank someone means to recognise their value. Narcissists find it extremely difficult to express these feelings. And, of course, sooner or later, the partner will simply get tired, as it becomes quite obvious why he is being used in this pair.

The narcissist is constantly swinging between idealisation and devaluation. He approaches you, another person whom he considers superior to himself, praising and singing glorifying serenades. There is so much flattery in his words that you begin to feel important and necessary. This is a huge trap in dealing with the narcissistic character.

This idealisation has nothing to do with your importance or need. The narcissist doesn't see the real you at all. Something about the way you present yourself temporarily blinded him. The very second you show your usual humanity, you will be totally devalued. Five minutes ago, you were the most beautiful, and now you are the most terrible.

The narcissist treats himself the same way. Either he idealises himself, and he is the most wonderful, or he devalues himself, and he is the most horrible. The key word here is "most". What is important is the grandiosity of this idealisation and devaluation. A narcissist does not have modest successes, he has great ones. But the narcissist does not experience simple everyday problems either. He can only suffer grandiosely and compete with others in who is sicker and who is more unhappy. This is a man who lives for the image. This image replaced his essence in childhood, and now he is full of exhibitionism, aloofness, emotional unavailability, fantasies of his own omnipotence and a constant tendency to condemn all the people around him.

## Need

If we're talking about the deepest need of the narcissist, then, of course, all they want is to relax. It seems that someone should allow them to be themselves and not try so hard, and then everything would be fine. Only, the moment for this has been irretrievably lost. The narcissist cannot be himself because he has never been himself. He has no idea what he is. Inside him, it is pitch dark and empty. If his achievements are taken away from him, if this beautiful facade is destroyed, then the narcissist will simply die psychologically.

Therefore, he will desperately defend himself against anything ordinary, against talk about humanity.

This is the second dangerous client for a tarot practitioner, and we will discuss later what you can and definitely shouldn't do when counselling a narcissist.

# SECTION 4. CORE TERM

## Regression

The concept of "regression" is the opposite of the concept of "progression". If we associate progress with development and qualitative advancement, then regression is when the opposite happens. In a psychological sense, there is a kind of rollback in development. It feels as if a person, unexpectedly for both themselves and those around them, is teleported in time to their past. Right now, we have before us, for example, not an adult, but a child, say, three to five years old.

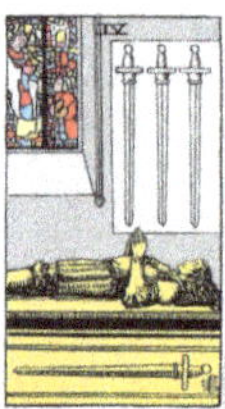

This description seems to suggest that this is a vivid phenomenon in the spirit of science fiction films, with all the accompanying special effects. But the trick is that psychological regression is most often so imperceptible that sometimes only a specialist can track it.

Let's try to understand where this phenomenon comes from. We have already talked about the fact that in our psyche there are a lot of unfinished psychological situations or centres of excitement that want to be discharged. These zones did not arise now, but in our past, most often in childhood. When an adult person finds themselves in a situation that the psyche recognises as similar to the one in which this excitement arose in the past, they begin to involuntarily, psychologically slide back to that very age.

Let's start with the most common example. Falling in love, especially the very beginning of a romantic relationship, is an extremely common regression. I think that everyone knows perfectly well what happens to a person who is in love. All their attention is occupied by their beloved person. If the partner responds, we have a huge amount of vivid bodily sensations. Phrases in the mind begin to crumble; they cannot even connect two words together. If the love is mutual, then the feeling of "I" disappears, and only one multi-coloured "we" appears. We idealise our partner: they are the best, the most beautiful, and we have a clear feeling that we simply cannot live without them. Doesn't it remind you of something? This is the typical psychological state of an infant who is in complete psychological confluence with his mother. The feelings are exactly the same. Psychologically, we are very similar to babies or children under three when we are in love.

There are less obvious examples. Suppose that a person has got into a new group, and naturally feels anxious, since he does not yet know anyone. He lacks social support, and he is much more vulnerable than usual. Two outcomes are possible. Either he'll urgently get acquainted with one of his colleagues in order to clarify the situation and get their support, or he'll "tightly stick" to the boss or leader of the group. We can understand whether there is a regression occurring or if an adult coping strategy is being used. In the first case, it is not a regression. This is a natural behaviour in a new group, enhanced by the excitement of not knowing anyone. But if an authority figure is needed for adaptation, then it is as if they have regressed to being a one-year-old, an age when babies explore the world around them, but constantly look back at their mothers. The world is still dangerous for them, and they do not yet have their own mechanisms for understanding who or what is around them. The emotional reaction and facial expression of the mother is the only measure that allows them to navigate the surrounding space. This regression makes a person very dependent and maladaptive.

Regression can also indicate a recurrence of a past trauma. If a person experienced situations that threatened their life as a child, then when they get scared now, they will mentally revert to the very age when the trauma happened. And their behaviour will correspond to this age. This could be a paralysis and a turning off of the psyche if the trauma was experienced in infancy. The behaviour may differ if the trauma was experienced at an older age, but it's still repetition and slippage. The psyche tries to defuse all the centres of excitation.

Regression is so common that it's hard to list all the potential examples. The range is simply huge: from the abstinence of a drug addict to a little more touchiness than usual on a birthday. I am sure that there are no people who have never experienced regression.

In the previous part of this book, we talked about transference. It is necessarily associated with regression, since the transference most often occurs with parental figures, or siblings, but also from the child's experience of the person. What should we do if we find ourselves in such a state?

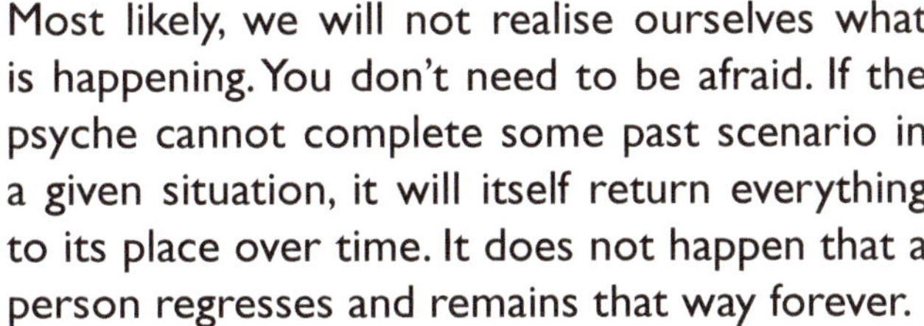

Most likely, we will not realise ourselves what is happening. You don't need to be afraid. If the psyche cannot complete some past scenario in a given situation, it will itself return everything to its place over time. It does not happen that a person regresses and remains that way forever.

In psychotherapy, regression occurs quite often, as the therapist constantly asks the client questions about their past. But the therapist is trained to notice these states and ask the client the question, "How old do you feel right now?" At first, the client freezes, as if convicted of something indecent. But then they notice that for some reason they really have been describing, for example, a quarrel with their friend as if they were not thirty, but thirteen years old. The subsequent clarification makes it clear that the client has regressed into adolescence and speaks of their friend like a sibling with whom they competed fiercely in adolescence.

Understanding the mechanism of regression can be very helpful for a tarot consultant. We deal with this all the time in our work. Just the unfamiliar format of tarot consultation itself can provoke a regression, if it was not explained to the client in advance what they were to participate in. Also, the very fact that some problem brought the client to the consultation also hints that they will be in regression. We all tend to slip into some earlier age when faced with impossible tasks, or when we are scared. Regression can also happen during a consultation. Since you are an authority figure attempting to help the client, parental transference to you is very likely. Of course, if this happens then you will not have a completely adult client in front of you, but partly a child who expects some parental function from you.

I can always identify when my clients are having regressive reactions, but some of my colleagues use the cards to help with this. There are many symbols in the deck that represent children. And if the client's question has nothing to do with children but these cards constantly appear in the spread, this is a hint that the client is in regression. Psychological training helps a lot in such situations because by the behaviour, facial expressions and speech of the client, one can understand what age period the client's psyche has slipped into, and what developmental task they are trying to solve.

# SECTION 5. THEORETICAL LECTURE

## Art Therapy

In this section, we will talk more about the beautiful than the terrible.

The concept of art therapy is directly related to creativity, which can also be an excellent psychological tool for work. Even without the recommendation of professionals, we are well aware that beauty has a very beneficial effect on our inner reality and harmonises our state. Sometimes, when confronted with great art, we are even able to experience real emotional catharsis and purification.

You may have noticed in films that when they show modern mental health facilities such as rehabilitation centres, psychiatric clinics or simply psychological self-help groups, there are usually patients' drawings on the walls, handicrafts they've made on display and photographs from various creative activities. There are no longer cages, straitjackets or lobotomy surgical tables. Today, a mental health institution is more like a children's creative centre, in which creativity is given the most important role. In many countries today, there are even laws against unnecessary hospitalisation of psychiatric patients, allowing them to live in society. This provides more chances for such patients to improve their condition, as the big society "pulls" them out of their pathology, allows them to feel part of it, to come into contact with the beauty and art of the big world.

Well, why do these patients or clients draw? Let's immediately clarify that we are not talking only about drawings. Art therapy today has a huge number of different directions.

First, there is music and vocal therapy. Music is an excellent way to work with the emotional sphere of a person. The sound has strong harmonising properties. There are masterclasses by specialists that are aimed at teaching clients to work with their own emotional state through singing and mastering their voice. Sometimes, through singing, a person manages to express some feeling, but with the proper degree of intensity. This has a similar effect to going to a deserted place in order to scream. A free and unrestrained cry helps to release a huge number of repressed feelings. Shouting among people is not always a good and harmless activity, and therefore, many people prefer not to do it in order not to attract undue attention to themselves—singing is an excellent alternative.

Where there is song, there is dance. Dance therapy is a huge area. We will talk more about this direction in the next book when we discuss body-oriented therapy and its trends. Here, though, we note that through movement a person can find a means for expressing and harmonising complex emotional states. Moreover, through dance we can reach the preverbal level of the psyche, since a dancer does not say anything in words, but tries to communicate with the outside world only through body language. It also includes the possibility of pair work, and therefore, the correction of partnerships. Dance therapy for couples can be an excellent tool for dealing with family crises as well as for developing interpersonal communication skills.

Fairy tale therapy is also a very interesting avenue of creative therapy. In the next book, we will talk about the narrative approach or paradigm in contemporary psychotherapy. Here, for now, we will simply say that the plots of various fairy tales can often be directly connected with us. These tales are often archetypal. We can identify with certain characters, merge with them, emotionally live through their experiences. Here, more often, we are not talking about classic fairy tales, but special fairy tales written by psychotherapists. Moreover, the client also gets the opportunity to write their own fairy tales about their own lives. In this case, the client will lead the plot themselves, turn it in any direction and thus "rewrite" not so much a biography, but an emotional map of past events.

It is not always possible to express some feelings on your own behalf. Sometimes it is much easier to put on the mask of a certain character. And here we have theatre as a therapeutic tool. There are also a large number of forms this can take. For example, puppet therapy is a way to work with some complex conditions, not on their own behalf but on behalf of the puppet that the client puts on their hand.

A very interesting technique is sand therapy. This is used with children when it is not only necessary to understand how the child perceives relationships with other people, but also to help them develop some new skills. In this technique, a small sandbox is located in the office of the therapist. It contains numerous small figurines.

The child is offered to choose these toys, to help them interact with each other. The psychologist understands which figure from the real life of the child is represented by each of the toys. This helps the psychologist to better understand what in psychology is called the sociometry of the child: who surrounds the child, and the relationships these people have with the child and each other.

In addition to these forms of creative therapy, there is also sculpture, and, in fact, drawing. We can talk about meditative drawing, when a person simply expresses themselves through a drawing and experiences certain feelings. But also, in psychology, there is a direction of psychodiagnostics which uses art to learn about a person. We can get a huge amount of information about a person when we observe what and how he draws. For example, there is the famous Tree-House-Man test. A person is asked to draw these three objects, and this provides us with excellent material for analysis. Children's drawings are also very informative. When a child draws his family, we can pay attention to how he arranges all family members in relation to himself. Who is holding hands, who is big and who is small, who is drawn in bright colours and who in dark. This is an excellent tool for exploring the inner world of a child.

Whatever means of self-expression we use in art therapy, we never evaluate our client's product in terms of its aesthetic value. They need to draw not professionally, but emotionally. No one will say that it is a bad or unsuccessful drawing. It needs to be interpreted, considered as material for psychological analysis and reflection, and not as an entry for a creative competition.

Art therapy, therefore, is an auxiliary, but very effective tool in general therapy. There are many areas in which it can be useful. First, it can be used to increase self-esteem. By itself, the non-evaluative technique of working with the client's product allows the client to experience unconditional acceptance. The client understands that they are not being judged for what they have drawn, but rather, they are being helped to understand what their drawing means and what makes it unique. Secondly, art therapy is an excellent way to work with stress, as a person gets a huge resource in the creative process, and learns to harmonise his state, which can help with depression or anxiety disorders. Creativity really helps us emerge from a deep emotional abyss. It provides a legal and correct way to act out heavy feelings or states. These are not always easy to put into words. Sometimes dancing or creating a sculpture helps better. The artist is very emotionally involved in the process, and as a result, part of their unbearable state ends up in the outside world, while inside it becomes much easier. Thirdly, art therapy also helps to develop communication skills. First, a person learns to express themselves through creativity, but then they transfer these self-expression skills into real-life conditions. Self-esteem grows, and it becomes easier for a person to talk about themselves with others.

Finally, of course, there are situations when art therapy becomes the therapist's only channel of access to a person and their inner states. When it comes to children, especially deeply disturbed children, it can be simply impossible to talk to them. This usual channel of communication has either not yet developed to the proper extent or has been broken due to trauma. How do we approach such a child? We can only play with them or draw. The child cannot describe their fear, but they can draw it. They cannot describe the episode of violence, but they can act it out with toys in the sandbox. This is how the child removes themselves from difficult experiences while telling the therapist something about what happened, so that the therapist can somehow help them. If we are talking about adults who cannot talk about their own feelings, then art therapy helps to develop what is called emotional intelligence. This allows the patient to be not only mentally intelligent, but aware of the smallest nuances of their state, and they develop a language that allows them to vocalise these states.

Child psychologists must master the use of art therapy as a tool. It is simply not possible to work with children otherwise. Sometimes it is impossible even to establish contact with a child other than through drawing or playing. But art therapy also gives good results when working with adult clients. Specialists usually mention elderly people in addition to children. With them, art therapy may also be the only available tool. Some of these clients are already cognitively impaired, and sometimes they simply cannot clearly explain what is happening to them. Art therapy also turns out to be a good tool for working with trauma (more about this in the third book). In treatment of post-traumatic stress disorder, art therapy techniques are used very actively.

In various books on tarot cards, we find recommendations to compose tarot albums ourselves or even draw our own deck. For the two classic decks of Rider-Waite and Thoth, professional artists were involved. But now, in my opinion, tarot is an interesting tool for art therapy to utilise. A huge number of decks have been created in which people conveyed their individual vision of those symbols present in the deck. There are examples of tarot theatre today. The symbols of tarot are present in design and fashion. They inspire and therefore can serve as a means of self-expression. This makes tarot stand out among all other mantic systems, as it is the most visual and oriented towards art and art therapy.

To work in the field of art therapy, you still need to be a professional psychologist. This cannot be done by any person without training. However, considering that there is already such an intensive integration of tarot and psychology, I am sure that in the near future we will get many professionals who will offer us new and interesting ways to work with tarot in the spirit of art therapy techniques. I think that everyone will benefit from this.

# SECTION 6. USEFUL TERMS

## MOTHER – FATHER – SIBLING FIGURE

On the one hand, all three—mum, dad, brother/sister—are close relatives; this is a family. But, on the other hand, our relationships with all three are completely different psychological experiences. We are not always aware of this, and sometimes it seems to us that everything depends on the character of these three figures, not their functions and tasks. Character, of course, is of great importance, but only in terms of how much it helps or hinders a child in getting what they need from these figures. In a father, mother and sibling, we get three basic models of relationships, on the basis of which we build all our future relationships, not only with individuals but with the whole world.

Of course, it all starts with the mother. She is the first person a baby interacts with after birth. The psyche of a baby is still in its infancy. The baby is absolutely merged with their mother and completely dependent on her. A person's development will depend on what experience they receive at the very beginning of interacting with the mother.

To begin with, the mother gives the child the experience of presence in this world. She is obliged to appear at any of the child's calls, to satisfy their needs. If she does this sensitively and correctly, then the whole world, which the mother personifies at this age, is seen as benevolent and safe. If the mother does not notice the child or carelessly handles the child's desires, this will have a far greater impact than it would for an adult. The child experiences this as a matter of life and death. The whole world has denied them the right to exist. This world is cold and hostile, it doesn't care about them, it doesn't welcome them. All this can be called the formation of basic human safety.

With the positive option, the child feels that they are noticed, that they are recognised and that they are celebrated. A good mother smiles at her child and talks to them affectionately. It is not so much the words that are important, but the tone and facial expressions. Through interaction with the mother, the child learns that someone can be attentive to their condition, that someone knows how to take responsibility for their comfort. The mother also provides an experience of emotional availability. A child at an older age should know that if they turn to their mother, then they will not be ignored. If the mother allows the child to separate from herself quite correctly and at the right time, but accepts the child back when they are frightened and doubting their independent abilities, the child receives the unique knowledge that their mother will be there, even when they do not feel her.

We have already discussed how important it is for a mother to correctly reflect her child and teach them the right emotional language. If everything is done correctly, then the child will not become a person prone to psychosomatic diseases. They will always be able to verbally describe their own state, and the body will not need to take on part of the load of the psyche in order to communicate with the outside world.

And, of course, the mother gives the child the experience of unconditional love and acceptance. Not all psychologists today agree that this love is so unconditional, hinting that the mother also receives something from the child. But in any case, no one in the world will love a child like their mother. That is why separation is such a difficult thing, and why regression is so attractive and relaxing. The power of maternal words is enormous, even over the psyche of an adult.

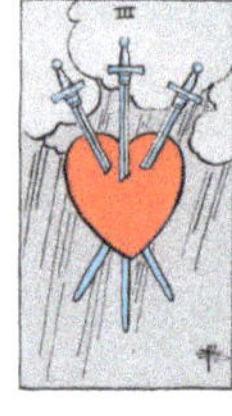

The fact is that the mother figure is the basis of our entire psyche; it is its foundation. And if the mother makes any unforgivable mistakes in childhood or is simply absent, there is a risk of getting such mental disorders that it will be impossible to correct in any way.

Dad is completely different! It's not that Dad cannot love a child, meet their needs and do the same as Mum—he certainly can—but with him, the child should get a completely different experience, which is no less important for a successful adult life. First, the father gives the child a sense of belonging. While the mother has been a presence in the child's life since before birth, the father appears in the child's zone of attention much later. *Who is this person?* the child wonders. *How does he relate to me, and how do I relate to him?* The child is disoriented by these questions. And when the father gives the child the message: "It's good that you are mine!", a very important need is fulfilled in the child's life. Now his kinship is recognised, and someone big and strong is taking responsibility for him. But then begins the process that radically distinguishes the father and mother in the experience of the child.

Usually, a lot of emphasis is placed on unconditional love. Of course, it is very nice to be loved no matter what you do. But for harmonious psychological development, conditional love is no less important. One of the tasks of the father is the socialisation of the child. He is the child's guide to the big world, which will definitely not love the child the way the mother did. For the child, at first it is a shock, since the father constantly wants something from them. It is important for him that the child grows up as a worthy and competent person. The father is especially attentive to the achievements of the child. And because of this, the child hears something like this from their father: "If you do something reasonable, then I will support you." The father takes responsibility for the future of the child; he is responsible for the social support of their efforts. Without this experience, it will not be possible to be successful in the big world.

And there is one more thing that only a father can do for a child. He makes the child understand that he, as a father, is responsible not only for his child, which would support the child's egocentric position, but also for other events and people. It is the father who pushes the child out of the egocentric belief that they are the centre of the universe. The child, albeit with sadness, or even with protest, understands that sometimes the father will be there, and sometimes he will go about his own business. The child doesn't expect that from a mother: she is always there and appears at the child's first call. But here it is completely different.

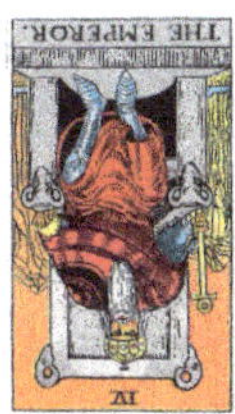

In my practice, I have very often seen examples when these two figures, in adulthood, begin to get confused, which can cause serious conflict. To begin with, let's establish that adult partners are not at all obliged to complete for the parents the work that did not go smoothly in childhood.

They can sometimes do this if they want and if the couple consciously agrees to do so. It often happens that an adult woman wants her man to take on a maternal position. She demands that he be always there, like a mother, that he be attentive to all her desires, like a mother, almost at the level of clairvoyance, and that he always be available for her wishes and needs. But a man identifies with his father in childhood, not with his mother. And he really has a lot to do besides maintaining this relationship. Such women cannot understand this and are very hurt when faced with a father's attitude instead of a mother's one. Some, with the help of pressure or manipulation, still succeed in making a mother out of their husband, but then they will often become disappointed with him after a while, as they no longer see masculinity in him.

And, of course, a few words must be said about siblings. Not all families have them. But for only children, this role is performed by other children in the neighbourhood, in nursery or just in the playground. However it happens, the child must gain experience in relationships with peers. This lays down many of the basic social mechanisms that will then work in adulthood. You need to learn to be friends, learn to compete, learn to negotiate and cooperate. Parents cannot give this experience to the fullest. Some parents are convinced that it is necessary to communicate with their children on an equal footing, to be friends with them. But let's admit that a child is not equal to an adult. When they speak of equality, they mean that they respect the child, not that the child is a fully fledged equal partner in a relationship. Moreover, the child does not need this from an adult. From an adult, the child wants protection, rules, clarity and admiration. An equal peer is needed for completely different things.

It has a positive effect on a person's development when they have experienced good examples of all three figures. Let's be clear right away: they don't need to be perfect, just good enough. Everyone makes mistakes—and by the way, those parents who strive for perfectionism often make many more mistakes out of anxiety. You just need to be a "good enough mum", not a perfect mum. Moreover, parents today have access to a huge amount of high-quality psychological resources that will help them navigate difficult situations during their child's upbringing.

If a person is not particularly lucky with any of these three figures, it's not the end of the world. But we must remember that the psyche will look for suitable figures in the environment and delegate to them those family functions that could not be completed in childhood. Sometimes you will be lucky, and, for example, a particularly empathetic teacher can give a student who grew up without a father a sense of professional acceptance, pride, conditional love and responsible social advice. But I would not recommend looking for such figures anywhere other than psychotherapy. A psychotherapist is a specialist who has been specially trained for such situations and who knows perfectly well what needs to be done. And the format of working with a psychotherapist will be long and stable, just as these relationships should be.

## Narcissistic Expansion

This term can be understood in two different ways. The first definition is that it is the use of the success and achievements of another person to raise one's own self-esteem. We considered examples of this in describing the narcissistic character, when a parent manipulates a child and sends the child to conquer the peaks in those areas in which the parent once failed themselves. This phenomenon will not necessarily occur in the parent-child relationship, it is just that a child is easier to control and manipulate. It can also occur in the configurations "husband-wife", "boss-subordinate" or "teacher-student".

The second definition is a slightly different situation. It can happen that a person receives praise or a greatly inflated assessment which absolutely does not correspond to reality. Again, this is manipulation. For example, a shop assistant who needs to sell a product will say that the buyer looks not just good in the suit they're trying on, but "grand". It is clear why this flattery and exaggeration is needed; the goal is to sell a product. Many buyers are well aware of the essence of this game, but willingly play it.

It is much worse when, in this way, they are trying to sell not a coat or a car, but a professional identity. Here the manipulations are not so obvious, but in my opinion, they are much more dangerous. For example, imagine a person needs to sell some long-term training course. Let's say it's training in psychotherapy. It is difficult to recruit a sufficient number of people in the group and keep them throughout the study. The salesman will tell prospective customers: "You are just a born psychologist! You will earn huge money! You see right through people! You simply cannot work badly in this profession!" Here, the consequences of such an expansion are much more devastating. The target is receiving praise from someone they already consider wise, experienced and professional. Most likely, a positive parental transference has already formed for such a teacher. And therefore, they really believe that all these qualities are inherent in them. They begin to learn this difficult profession. And then it turns out that they are average. Not only do they not have such talents as they were told at the beginning, it also turns out that this is not the profession for them at all. But it's very hard to get out. They've already spent a lot of time and money on training. They can't admit defeat now.

There are a lot of such seduced young professionals in every profession. Here, of course, those who lacked parental positive reflection in childhood are more vulnerable. These people will try to get it in adulthood. But it is important to be critical of such messages. What does it mean: "You just can't do bad work in this profession?" Everyone, even the highest-level professional, sometimes makes mistakes.

We're also discussing this topic here because some tarot practitioners actively use this narcissistic expansion in their work. The client, of course, will return again, if no one else has ever praised them so much in their life. But there is definitely an element of manipulation here, which will sooner or later be revealed, and the client will face a powerful disappointment.

## Identity

This, too, would seem to be a very frequently used word, but not everyone understands its essence.

Let's start with the fact that a person always has several identities, and they are acquired and abandoned in the process of constant identification and separation. It all starts in early childhood, when the baby has just been born, and there is a gradual formation of their personality.

At first, the child is completely identified with those figures who care for them. The child is part of the parents, and the parents are part of the child. Then, a little later, the child usually begins to realise that they are a boy or a girl and identifies themselves with the parent of the same sex. The child has a growing family identity. They understand that these two are their parents, this is their house and this is their room. That is, the child's idea of themselves acquires more and more new characteristics. Then the child learns to be part of children's groups. They understand that here is their nursery, here is their school and class, and here is the church where their family are parishioners. The child understands that they belong to a certain religious denomination, understands that they speak this and not another language, realises that they live in this particular country, which leads them to the formation of a cultural and national identity.

Separation occurs when one of the identities begins to interfere with development. For example, it is impossible to acquire adult identity without separation from parents. During the teenage crisis, the child devalues their parents and becomes part of a group of peers. This group identity is needed to experiment with adulthood. Only later, when this period ends and a romantic partner is found, is the person separated from the teenage group, and the corresponding identity, and becomes an adult.

And then there is the acquisition of a professional identity, the identity of a parent when their own children are born, and so on. Of course, this process is slow and gradual. You cannot simply declare yourself, for example, a pianist and immediately acquire the identity of a musician.

For this, others are needed who have the same identity and give the person acceptance and the right reflection.

How do I know that I am a tarot reader? On the one hand, I know the craft and have been practising for a long time. But on the other hand, the world recognises this professional identity of mine: clients come to me, colleagues consider me "one of them"; I have published books and articles on this topic.

In the next book, we will talk more about developmental crises as points where a person's identity goes through qualitative changes. This is always very painful, as the person temporarily experiences disorientation, and cannot clearly and distinctly answer one of the most important questions: "Who am I?" The old identity no longer works, and the new one has not yet formed. This happens not only during periods of age crises but also at moments of serious life changes—for example, when a person in middle age decides to completely change their profession. This is very difficult to do because in addition to new knowledge, you also need to form a new professional identity. Immigration is also a good example of such a transformation. In fact, crises such as these are often one of the things that bring clients to tarot consultations, and tarot readers have to work with people in a similar state.

## Self-Agression

The topic of self-aggression is very extensive, and we will touch on it only very superficially, simply listing its main types and forms. Separately, in the third book of this series, we will talk in more detail about suicidal behaviour as its extreme form, since it is important for a tarot consultant

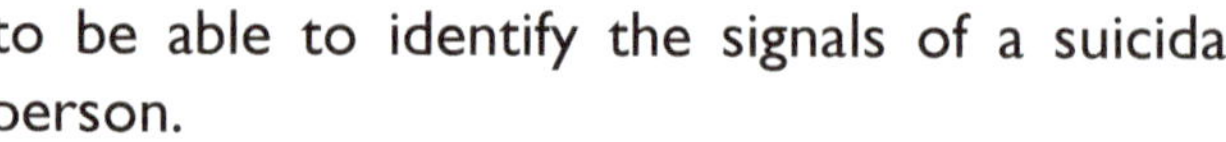

to be able to identify the signals of a suicidal person.

In general, this mechanism can be explained very simply. These are situations when aggression, which is addressed to the outside world, cannot be expressed, for any reason, and then the person turns it against themselves.

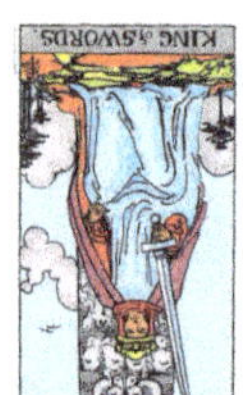

There are so many forms of this that sometimes people do not even realise that they are showing self-aggression because it is something many people do, and sometimes it is even supported by culture. On the mental level, it can be self-blame, self-abasement and obsessive thoughts. At the behavioural level, this is direct self-harm, which can manifest in many ways, from getting piercings and tattoos to alcoholism and drug addiction to actually killing oneself.

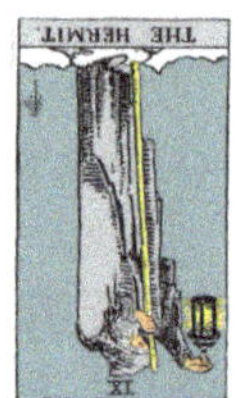

Various reasons can underlie such behaviour and thinking. Of course, the wrong upbringing can be to blame for everything, if the child experienced humiliation and criticism more often than love and protection. It may be actual abuse that has caused the trauma. It can happen that people with too punishing a super-ego will choose a mystical or religious tradition involving asceticism, suffering and self-restraint. If someone experiences great difficulties in an inherently competitive work environment, it is not always possible for them to openly express their aggression in conflicts, since they are at risk of losing their job. And, of course, self-aggression can be a tool of manipulation, if a person harms themselves in order to receive attention and care.

The reasons can be completely different in every case. The problem is that the unconscious nature of self-aggression can greatly reinforce it,

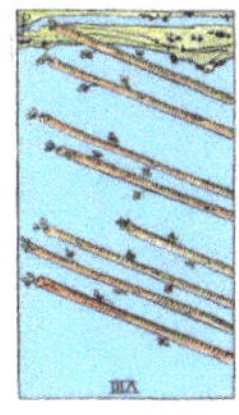

and people often simply do not realise the line where a harmless diet becomes self-torture, or they start a series of endless plastic surgeries that are really life-threatening. The tarot consultant needs to see these patterns, and if they are excessive, clarify them in consultation with the client. Perhaps the client just needs a safe space to act out their aggression.

## Projection

Projection is a psychological defence mechanism, which we will discuss in detail in the second book of the series. This mechanism is so common that I decided to describe it a little earlier. The essence of projection is that a person splits off from themselves some characteristic, the awareness of which threatens their positive self-esteem, and transfers or projects it onto someone else. This gives them the opportunity, on the one hand, to experience this feeling, albeit indirectly, through contact with another, while on the other hand, maintaining a positive self-image in their mind.

There really are a lot of examples of this. "It's not that I hate people, it's that they hate me." "It's not me who lusts for this man, he sexually pursues me." "It wasn't me who was offended, you were offended and looking at me in a strange way." Projection often legitimises some pattern of behaviour, such as retaliatory aggression. It's hard for a person to just admit that he doesn't like someone and attack them. If he does this, he considers himself negatively. But accusing another person of aggression and attacking them allegedly out of self-defence is another matter. Protecting yourself is a very noble thing.

In tarot counselling, we encounter projections all the time. The client is not aware when they are projecting. Very often it occurs in situations of pathological jealousy. For example, a client may be obsessed with the idea that her husband is cheating on her. This may indeed be true, but it often happens that she herself feels a strong sexual dissatisfaction and is about to be ready for adultery. The realisation of this would be absolutely detrimental to her self-esteem, so she will blame her husband instead. In subsequent books, we will discuss whether it is worth making the client aware of their projections and interpreting them, or if it is better to remain silent. Each case is completely individual. Therefore, we will continue to discuss other topics in order to gain more material, and then we will return to the issue of interpreting psychological defences.

## Sublimation

Sublimation is also a psychological defence mechanism, only, perhaps, one of the most mature and useful. Sometimes, it is even used intentionally because it can be used to help cope with difficult situations, although, in this case, it has partly ceased to be a defence, and is, instead, a way of acting out.

Those impulses and instincts that are socially punishable are subject to sublimation, primarily violence and sexuality. They can be combined under one concept of "aggression", if we understand it broadly, as it is accepted in psychology. It is impossible to openly kill a person, so you can find a close, but socially acceptable occupation, such as surgery. The surgeon really cuts people, but he does it in such a way that everyone only benefits from it. Also, sport is an excellent sublimation area. Instead of both countries starting a war against each other with many casualties and destruction, you can meet on the football field or basketball court and replace the war with a competition.

There are also many examples of sublimation of sexual drive—for example, any creative self-expression that includes elements of eroticism. Creativity has a unique ability to connect and express absolutely any impulse in a person and give them socially approved forms. On the stage, you can act any play, the plot of which does not need to be experienced in real life at all. And when a person, whether on stage or in the auditorium, is immersed in this performance, they experience the same feelings that they would if the scenario unfolded in real life.

We remember that everything is always more obvious from the outside than from the inside of a situation. Sometimes, for some reason, it doesn't occur to the client that you can go to the gym and beat a punching bag, and not your boss. The tarot consultant sometimes really has to remind the client of the wonderful alternative that is: sublimation.

# SECTION 7. REFLECTION ON A PRACTICAL CASE

## EMPRESS TAKES OFF HER CROWN, CHAPTER 4

Emma stood silently in the corridor for about half an hour. A sudden phone call brought her to her senses, causing her to jump. She pressed the button and saw her new neighbour friends on the screen.

"Hi!" Liz and Tom said in unison.

"Hi!" Emma replied. "What time is it now?"

"Already six. Have you finished? Are you coming to us?" Tom asked.

Emma fluttered sharply. She began to run around the apartment like she'd overslept for work and had only five minutes, instead of an hour, to get everything sorted. But what did she need, in this case? She just needed to take a bottle of wine from the refrigerator and turn off the light in the apartment. What had got her so flustered? Realising this, Emma froze in place, as if rooted to the spot. She felt completely uneasy, and she asked:

"Liz, can you run to my place for a minute? I need some help."

"Of course," Liz replied. "Just me, or should Tom come too?"

"No." Emma blushed. "Just you, please. It's just some kitchen stuff."

"Did you cook something?" Tom asked. "Hey, I love all kinds of bakes."

"I'm on my way," Liz said and hung up the call.

Emma grabbed her head. *God, what am I doing?*

Liz arrived right away. Emma opened the door for her and literally pulled her into the apartment by the collar, looking around warily to see if Tom had followed her.

"Well, what are you doing?" Liz asked. "Where is the cake?"

"There is no cake!" Emma hissed, still whispering, as if someone might be eavesdropping. "I just wanted to ask you—did you tell Tom that I went for coffee with John this morning?"

Liz thought for a moment.

"No, I didn't. It seems... Wait." She fell silent, trying to figure out something in her mind. "No, I didn't say for sure. What is it?"

Emma herself did not understand what exactly was happening. It was as if she had simultaneously lost all control of all her faculties. Thoughts were confused, and all feelings were mixed in one powerful flurry. Her hands were trembling, and tears flowed from her eyes.

"I'm such a fool!" she said, sobbing. "I acted like a haughty bitch with John this morning."

"What are you talking about?" Liz was worried.

"I sat like an employer at an interview. I looked at him in such a superior way, as if he were some kind of nonentity. Like I'm so cool, he's just a janitor at school. I'm sorry—he's your friend."

Liz was completely confused. She took Emma into the study, patting her on the back, and sat with her on the sofa.

"Wait," she said. "First of all, he's Tom's friend, not mine. We just work at the same school. Secondly, he's not a janitor. Why did you think so? He is a gym teacher. And it's not like he's royalty—you don't need to treat him specially. Who cares?"

Emma continued to sob. Her thoughts were beginning to line up again, and it all became a little clearer in her head.

"But you wanted to introduce us. And I ruined everything. He must have thought that I..."

Liz ran her hand over her forehead. "Look, it's not a big deal—I just thought it might work. His mother is an astrologer. I thought you'd have something to talk about; I don't think that stuff's really for him though. Just a nice guy—and single. I thought you might like him. He and Tom go to the gym together. Tom says he's a cool guy, a little lonely. We have half the school crushing on him. I don't really talk to him at work, but it turned out that he was training Tom, and that they are friends. Tom told me a lot about him. That's where I got interested."

Emma felt like she was about to sink into the floor from shame. Liz looked at her friend in bewilderment, not knowing what else to say. It was obvious that she herself was embarrassed.

She tried to calm Emma. "I probably shouldn't have. I didn't think you'd react like that. You understand that I am not your mother or grandmother, right? I'm definitely not trying to marry you to some enviable gentleman. Although, to be honest, I was stupid. I should have invited him to something with all four of us. I didn't think about what it might look like. But you do realise that you don't owe anyone anything, don't you?"

Liz's phone suddenly rang.

"Are you alright there?" Tom asked worriedly.

"No! Yes!" Liz answered stubbornly. "We've dropped this… cake."

She blurted out the first thing that came to her mind, looking worriedly at Emma and making some conspiratorial gestures that only she could understand.

"Damn, sorry!" Tom said. "Well, it's not a problem. Can I help you?"

"No, no," Liz said. "We'll clean up here and come back."

Emma was suddenly seized with intense anxiety. She jumped up from the sofa, ran to the kitchen, took out a bag of flour from the cupboard and put her hand inside.

"What are you doing?" Liz asked in bewilderment, running into the kitchen after her.

Emma, meanwhile, ran her hand over her cheeks. They were wet with tears, so the flour began to roll into lumps. Now Emma really looked ridiculous, as if she had survived an explosion in a bakery. Hands trembling, she almost dropped the bag of flour, and she squeezed it awkwardly, causing a white cloud of flour to splatter her blouse.

"That's to make it natural," Emma blathered nervously. "About the cake. Don't say anything to Tom."

"Stop it! I've never seen you like this before." Liz became angry. "What difference does it make what he thinks? He will trust what we tell him. Wipe your face and let's go. As for John, forget it! You don't owe anyone anything. We are all adults here. If you want, you can meet him again. If you don't want to, you shouldn't do anything. It doesn't really matter. Next time, I'll also be smarter. Probably, somewhere, I pressed this on you; there was no need to show such zeal. We should've met as a group, and that's it."

Emma hid the bag of flour and began to wash her face. She managed to wash off the worst of it, but remnants were still on her hair and clothes. They left the apartment, taking with them a bottle of wine from Emma's refrigerator. Tom opened the door for them and looked in surprise at his wife and neighbour.

"Everything okay?" he asked, looking at Emma. "Did you drop the cake on yourself?"

"Yeah, that's how it was," Liz said quickly. "It doesn't matter, forget about the cake, damn it! Come on, come on." She literally pushed Emma into her apartment.

It wasn't the first time they'd got together like this. They didn't always want to go out somewhere in the city, so it was much easier to meet up at one of their flats. Tom and Liz's apartment was cosy and warm, and they'd sit and talk about anything. Being with friends, Emma sometimes forgot that she was visiting—she sometimes felt more relaxed, more comfortable and safe than she did at home. But today, even an hour later, Emma was still on pins and needles, as if she had been undressed in front of a large crowd of people. Tom definitely noticed, but he seemed to read his wife's thoughts and did not ask another uncomfortable question. He acted as if he couldn't see the flour stains on Emma's clothes, her tear-stained eyes, or hear the tension in her voice.

But gradually, the atmosphere of a warm, friendly evening brought Emma to her senses.

*Damn, what was it?* Emma tried to explain her own behaviour and reaction to the day's events to herself.

After all, nothing had gone wrong that morning, but she seemed to have fallen back to somewhere in early childhood, when she'd had to perform on stage at school and had prayed that her parents would not come to watch her performance. She'd been ready to dance in front of anyone, but not in front of them. Her father always looked at her like a strict judge and then tried to sort out her mistakes with her. Emma couldn't stand it. Other children were glad that their parents came to see them, and their parents reacted differently, always with tenderness and joy, no matter how their child performed. Emma envied them.

She thought back to that morning and coffee with John. No, she hadn't been rude to him. She'd just looked distant and not particularly interested. It might have looked like she was tired and hadn't had enough sleep.

Emma tried to remember what John looked like. He really was handsome. Not like Brian, her client of a couple of hours ago—that one was like the cover of her father's magazine. John was more like an ordinary guy, very natural and free. Emma remembered that she'd felt at that moment that the whole coffee shop was watching them. Or had they just been looking at John? Emma had felt a little uneasy. He had said nothing about himself at all, as Emma now remembered. He'd asked her about her work, her clients, her interests. Then she'd had to run, so she didn't really ask anything about him.

Thinking about it that way, that coffee did not seem so ugly to her, or her behaviour haughty. She even wanted to rehabilitate herself and continue the conversation with John.

She followed Liz into the kitchen a little later as she carried the empty glasses through.

"Listen, thank you," she said in a whisper. "I seem to have let go. I was probably just overworked."

"I thought so," Liz said in a whisper, too.

"I think I'll see John again," Emma said.

"Hey, hey, wait." Liz got worried. "Are you sure you want to? You definitely shouldn't just because—"

Emma interrupted her. "No, I want to. I don't think I talked enough with him. I'll call him and invite him myself. Something makes me curious about him."

Liz nodded silently, handed her friend a bowl of fruit, and they returned to Tom in the living room.

# SECTION 8. PRACTICAL RECOMMENDATIONS

## Practical Analysis of Chapters 3 and 4

Well, here he is, a really dangerous client for a tarot consultant. And as we can see, the danger does not necessarily unfold in full during the consultation itself. Quite often it happens that the narcissist leaves behind a very toxic residue, which the consultant has to digest for a long time. This is exactly what happened in Emma's case. But let's talk about everything in order.

1. First of all, you should pay attention to how the client looks. Narcissists are indeed much more concerned about their appearance than other characters. Emma noticed that the client looked like a model from the cover of a magazine. This is not necessarily proof that we are dealing with a narcissist. But if we add coldness, formality, some arrogance, as well as tension in the figure, then such an assumption becomes a little more likely. From the narcissist there always breathes an unnatural beauty, and this is usually felt when in contact with them.

2. It is very important to understand how strong a narcissistic radical is present in the character of the practitioner as well. Emma had a very difficult childhood, as well as past experience in a narcissistic business environment. The fact that she left there suggests that she was able to find what makes her herself, so she cannot be called a classic narcissist. But her narcissistic period was not lived out correctly by her as a child. This makes her a little more vulnerable when dealing with narcissistic clients. She will react much more strongly to idealisation and devaluation, as we saw.

3. As we discussed earlier, narcissists are constantly sliding between two poles—idealisation and devaluation. They approach people in the same way. Brian did just that. This was noticeable

from his first opening speech. Emma felt tense, and this partly saved her. Had she completely succumbed to his flattery, then the devaluation would have been much more severe. But the client still managed to knock her off balance. Emma's initial vigilance was nevertheless lulled by the way Brian reacted to her accurate interpretations. This usually happens so subtly that it is very difficult to track exactly how the client narcissistically extends the practitioner. It is also difficult to resist this because it is always very pleasant. Not all clients are so generous with feedback. Plus, esotericists often live with a sense of chronic social devaluation and find it difficult to maintain a positive professional self-image. Therefore, they tend to respond especially strongly to someone praising them. But something else is important here.

4. Positive feedback and the idealisation of a narcissist are two different things. The second is completely pointless. The healthy narcissist within us fills up when we receive positive feedback matching our own achievements, but in the case of a narcissist, their praise is always either exaggerated or inadequate to the situation. It's nice when they say that you work miracles. But Emma herself did not consider her work miraculous. Therefore, Brian's praise did not match her inner feelings. Plus, this was the first time she'd met him. They just hadn't interacted enough for him to appreciate Emma's work properly.

And as we already know, devaluation always follows idealisation. But it can happen in two ways.

5. Most often, some time passes between idealisation and devaluation. Usually, when working with a narcissist, a tarot reader gets addicted to the feeling of being great, incomparable and infallible. And only after some time, will they abruptly be brought back from heaven to earth. The client may do this on the fourth or fifth visit, as, at first, he still needs a figure to idealise, and a tarot practitioner is very suited to this role. But it can also occur, as in Emma's case, almost immediately. In my opinion, the client's attitude swung so sharply because Emma did not buy into his idealisation much. If she'd begun to praise herself, talk about her successes or, as many tarologists do, begin to overestimate the merits of the cards aloud, then the client would not have immediately moved on to devaluation. But Emma tried to work with him, let's say, humanly, which led to their subsequent dynamic.

6. Note that narcissists often ask questions about a project. Usually, this is some kind of work situation. Even if the question concerns the topic of relationships, then the narcissist will look at everything from the point of view of their own image. Brian immediately made it clear that he was not particularly interested in people. This was evident in his comments regarding colleagues at work. Emma's mistake was not that she began to promote the option of relocation to Poland—which she didn't actually do, by the way—but that she began to promote a dangerous value (Brian's girlfriend), which was clearly not a priority for the client. Moreover, the narcissistic client is very afraid of feeling shame. I think that talking about relationships just pushed Brian into this forbidden pole. He had not mentioned this topic at all himself, which means that it is not part of his narcissistic facade. Emma should not have gone into this area at all, since the client did not request it. Here, she was right to believe she'd made a mistake, but her reaction to the error was already poisoned by the malignant narcissistic dynamics. She fell into thick shame and self-depreciation.

7. But then there is an ethical question. Isn't it necessary to tell the client what you see in the cards, even if the client does not ask? I have two answers to this question. Information about events definitely does not need to be voiced without a request. But it is sometimes useful to show that there is a connection between topics, even if the client hasn't asked about one of them. Brian is an exception to this rule. Narcissists are very different from other clients. Quite often, narcissistic clients will have a healthy degree of narcissism. They will be adaptable and have access to the strategies of other character types, but they will still be reluctant to talk about something that does not make them look perfect. Here, the practitioner must exercise extreme caution. We must look at how empty the client is inside, and how important they consider their true desires. That is, if success outweighs the client's desire to be themselves, then there is no need to introduce unnecessary topics into the consultation. The client will devalue such an attempt by the practitioner. Brian even explicitly said that his own desires were not important at all, which gave Emma a hint that it was not necessary to go into these forbidden topics. She, unfortunately, did not pay heed to it.

8. It is very good that Emma did not shame the client for choosing a career at the expense of his girlfriend's well-being. For

narcissists, this would be unbearable. They come for a consultation in order to be reflected in their beauty and grandeur in the eyes of a tarologist, who they also idealise due to the peculiarities of their status (after all, they are the herald of the Higher Forces). Such a reflection gives them huge positive reinforcement. They are generally not in the mood to hear criticism and even less willing to experience shame for something. This is also one of the reasons why they are such difficult clients: the practitioner must constantly filter what they are saying. Such clients should not be frustrated, but sometimes in our work frustration is necessary. Narcissists won't let the tarot reader do that. As soon as they feel a threat to their ideal external facade, they will immediately swing the whole process towards devaluation, and everything will be over quickly.

9. Brian devalued Emma in a very unusual way. He didn't say anything hurtful to her. But the fact that he requested a consultation at an inconvenient time, then extended Emma so narcissistically with positive comments and praise, and then abruptly terminated the consultation, is also a form of devaluation. He did not say "thank you" to her at the end, which is also characteristic of narcissists. The client first symbolically let her know that she was needed, and then by his behaviour showed her exactly the opposite. The phrase "this just isn't for me" seems to have been said by Brian regarding himself, but in the end, it could be addressed to Emma, too. These matters weren't for her, either; it was she who could not correctly tell the client what was more important to him.

10. Now, about the toxic residue after the consultation. Emma lived it to the fullest. Here, there was a real regression to a childish state in which Emma felt shame. This is exactly what clients with a narcissistic radical most often do: they evacuate their own pole of worthlessness, badness and shame into the practitioner. Usually, after working with a narcissist, a tarot reader has the feeling that they are a bad tarot reader. They begin to feel ashamed of their incompetence; it seems to them that they have read the cards incorrectly. Maybe they even begin to feel that their appearance was flawed. It begins to seem to the tarologist that they smelled unpleasantly, that they were somehow untidily dressed or that their voice was unpleasant. This pole of one's own inferiority is also lived in a narcissistic way, that is, to the maximum extent. The tarot reader not only made a mistake; they made an unforgivable

and deadly mistake. They did not simply frustrate the client but caused irreparable harm. Not only did they not work well, but their cards should be taken away and they should be banned from approaching people forever. This is always experienced very painfully, and everyone emerges from this regression at different speeds. Emma, thanks to the support of her friends, managed to come to the surface quickly enough, but for many novice practitioners, a serious professional crisis can begin after such an experience at work.

11. As you can see, a narcissist is a very harmful client. The problem is that there are a lot of them. This character radical is extremely widespread today, especially in the Western world. A tarot reader must be prepared for the fact that a narcissistic client will definitely hit the tarologist's own narcissistic strings. This is painful for experienced tarot readers and can be downright devastating for beginner practitioners whose professional identity is still in dire need of positive feedback. Nevertheless, if a narcissist comes to see you, remember that you are already limited in your abilities. You will not be allowed to show yourself correctly for two reasons: either you will not be able to talk about the unpleasant sides of the client, or you yourself will be knocked out of a stable professional position and made to doubt your own competence.

# SECTION 9. TRAPS AND DANGERS

## Realising the Limitations in the Work of the Tarot Reader

I do not think there is any area of activity that can cover all the possible needs of a person. If that were the case, we wouldn't need so many professions. Esotericism cannot do what art can do. Tarot cannot do what astrology does.

Understanding the topic of tarot's limitations is useful for two reasons. First, practitioners must be aware of the limits of their capabilities and of their system. Secondly, from an ethical point of view, it is useful to convey this to the client.

Inexperienced clients who know nothing about what the cards are and what they are capable of will be inclined to look at the tarot as an all-powerful tool. They are lured into consultations by esoteric ideas from their own world view, which are usually very naive, and even childish. We remember how children look at their parents. In a child's eyes, the parent has all the most positive characteristics that a child's fantasy is capable of. Clients, while in regression, will also tend to see in the tarot reader or in the cards some unique tool that can work wonders.

Inexperienced and novice tarologists also tend to idealise their own working tool. It takes a long time for the proper disappointment to occur, naivety to be replaced by maturity, and the tarologist to ground their attitude towards their work. Some people simply cannot stand such frustration and give up the practice. But if they persist with it, what do they begin to understand? The following list is by no means comprehensive, but I hope it will inspire you to think about the topic further on your own.

Firstly, tarot readers realise that what they predict is definitely not a rigid future and not a fate that has already been prescribed by someone. They deal with a variant future that will only happen if the client does not change anything in their present. Quite often it turns out to make a fairly accurate prediction, but it is not always clear what made the prediction accurate. Perhaps it was something fateful. Perhaps the client simply agreed with this version of the future and created it for themselves, since everything suited them. Perhaps the client was dissatisfied with the forecast, but did not have enough time to change in the present in order to change their future. The tarologist should remember that the system does not always make 100 percent accurate predictions. The cards show trends, although they do it quite well.

Secondly, it is still not clear what exactly determines the accuracy of forecasts and interpretations. Some tarot readers simply cannot answer some questions. The question itself can cause such a strong rejection in the practitioner that the practitioner cannot separate themselves from their own experience, focus on the client's situation and read the spread correctly. Gradually, it becomes necessary to make a list of taboo questions.

Thirdly, tarologists quickly realise that they have a problem with predicting specific time periods, and especially dates. Tarot works strangely with time. The flow of time in the tarot itself is somehow different from that in ordinary life. If the client asks for a date and the tarologist answers, it most often turns out to be incorrect. The tarologist described exactly what would happen, but seriously missed the time period. Some clients will say that exactly the opposite happens with astrologers. They say the dates quite accurately, but they give such an abstract description of the event that nothing is clear. The client angrily says: "I wish I could find a practitioner that combines these two systems." Tarot readers begin to understand that for successful work, they cannot work with cards alone, and they begin to master related disciplines: astrology, numerology, runes or psychology. Practice itself makes them constantly develop, as it puts before them more and more new tasks.

Fourthly, it turns out that cards sometimes downright deliberately push a person into an unpleasant experience. The tarot reader correctly read the spread, but when the client followed the advice, they got the opposite outcome. The client is angry and dissatisfied and makes a complaint to the tarologist. And then it turns out that the client needed to get into such a problem, otherwise they would not have learned some important lesson for themselves. Not all clients admit this, but sooner or later the tarologist must conclude that the cards do not serve the human ego. They work for the benefit of the client's Higher Self, whatever you call it. The problems and desires of the earthly personality are of secondary importance. If a person has a strong imbalance of their higher and lower nature, then the cards can "set them up". Who, then, is be responsible for this?

Fifthly, there is an idea that the client's general anxiety will decrease a little because they can see what others think and feel about them. But think again! The cards show something strange. They do not truly show the thoughts of anyone but the client, but rather a reflection of other people in the unconscious of the client. It's like astrologers say: "In a person's horoscope, there is neither Mum, nor Dad, nor God, nor the devil. There is only the person himself with his individual perception of Mum, Dad, God and the devil." Another frustration. Over time, the tarot reader realises how important this perspective is, and this awareness comes only with experience.

I am sure that every tarologist can list a number of other limitations that they face in their work. It is important that these limitations are realised and voiced to the client. If the tarot reader does not think about what is actually available to them and what is not, what they are useful for, and in which situations it is better to redirect the client to another specialist, such a practitioner becomes similar to the manic character that we talked about in the first part of this book.

# SECTION 10. PSYCHOLOGICAL PARADIGM

## TRANSACTIONAL ANALYSIS

Let's imagine that our psyche is arranged like a theatre in which various actors perform certain roles and play out certain scenarios. This metaphor is the best way to help us understand what the transactional analysis paradigm is. Eric Berne, the creator of this paradigm in psychotherapy, proposed distinguishing three states of the ego in our psyche. He named them the Child, the Parent and the Adult.

The Child is the part that acts impulsively and spontaneously and is not guided by the principles of reason and logic. It acts like a child of up to about eight years old who is a source of humour and creativity. Here, it is necessary to make a reservation that this inner Child can be different for each person. In one case, it will be a natural and spontaneous child who enjoys life. In another case, we will get an obedient child who already has some control over his inner activity. In any case, this Child is not taken from thin air. It is exactly the child that the person was in childhood, with their inherent characteristics and character traits.

The Parent, of course, is a completely different matter. This is the state of the ego that is responsible for control and limitations in our lives. The Parent is also the guardian of values and traditions and is very important in allowing a person to be part of society and live among other people. The Child is not capable of this; they are too chaotic. The Parent is also a kind of sum of all the authoritative figures from a person's childhood. These are parents, grandparents, as well as numerous educators. Like the Child, the Parent is different for each person. The Parent can be careful and caring, or critical or indifferent, a Parent-Pig (as the creators of transactional analysis themselves put it).

The Adult is not some summary figure from a person's past. It is some kind of analytical centre in our psyche, a logical computer that analyses what happens to the person and helps to make certain decisions.

At different points, one of the ego states will enter the scene and begin to dominate. The Child forces a person to be spontaneous and playful; they ask for pleasure and play and push for creative solutions. It is the most energetic ego state. On the other hand, when the Child comes forward, a person may feel helpless and defenceless, become vulnerable and not know how to competently cope with this or that situation. Then the Parent can come to the fore, which will make a person become serious and authoritative, solve some difficult problem or provide support to someone. Then the Adult appears when you need to orient yourself in a certain situation, analyse it and draw conclusions. Then the Parent again, then the Child, then the Adult, etc.

It is good if these states show themselves in appropriate situations, but it often happens that at the very moment the Parent is needed, the Child appears, who cannot do anything useful. Or, on the contrary, a person might find themselves, for example, in the company of friends, where everyone is relaxed and enjoying themselves, and not be able to relax in any way. Instead of the Child, who is needed now, the moralising Parent dominates. And then the person begins to boringly lecture everyone, which quickly spoils the atmosphere for them all.

One of the tasks in transactional analysis is to learn how to regulate these switches. It can happen that a person's Child is so persecuted and deprived of the right to speak up that it takes a lot of time and effort in therapy to revive this ego state. Without a healthy Child, one can forget not only about pleasure but also the very principle of vitality and love of life, since it is the Child who is responsible for such things. Sometimes you need to moderate the ardour of the Parent, who can be unnecessarily dominant and punishing. These things are usually connected—a downtrodden and lethargic Child and a despot Parent. Or, on the contrary, the Parent can be so irresponsible that the Child has no restrictions. This also promises problems, since such a person will have all their safety parameters knocked down and, like a child, will constantly get into trouble because they do not feel the boundaries of what is permitted. Such a person may also have significant difficulties in social adaptation, since the Child does not accept it, and the Parent does not care what happens.

There can also be significant problems in interpersonal communication when a message from the ego state of one person switches on an inadequate ego state in the second. For example, a wife flirts with her husband and seduces him (her inner Child is at work, sending a message to the husband's inner Child). But for some reason, the husband begins to lecture or criticise her; that is, he responds with the Parental part. There are many such examples of communication failure.

These ego states do not motivate a person towards any activity; they are structural components. But speaking of motivation, transactional analysis suggests paying attention to the following needs. First, there is a hunger for stimulus and for recognition. It is appropriate to say here that people need to constantly interact with others, otherwise sensory deprivation may occur, which has a very bad effect on the individual. This is why isolation is so painful, and the psyche will agree even to cruel treatment to avoid facing total isolation. Recognition by others is positive feedback, which we also really need. We are constantly interacting with others to receive these strokes.

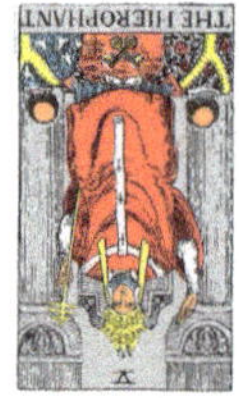

Secondly, people need to structure their time. Their lives should be filled with eventful certainty. Therefore, we need rituals, participation in the life of various social institutions, and labour.

To meet these needs, people constantly enter into various transactions, or short episodes of interaction. They unknowingly play games with each other that have a specific goal and a fee to participate. A classic example of such a game is "What if you…?" "Yes, but…" This is a game in which one person complains about a certain problem, and others join in and begin to suggest solutions. But whatever they offer, the instigator of the game rejects all options. The participants paid the price, and the instigator established his position: that his problem is the most problematic problem in the world (the narcissistic goal of the game).

Because of the need to structure time, we often tend to conceptualise our lives as consisting of certain fixed scenarios. Usually, these scenarios are not invented anew each time but are taken ready-made, borrowed from the cultural treasury. There is an opinion that there are a limited number of such scenarios, so it is difficult to write something new, truly revolutionary, today. For example, in the plot of the film *Pretty Woman* we see elements of Pygmalion; Hamlet has something in common with the myth of Oedipus. It is myths and fairy tales that are most often such stencils, according to which we unconsciously build our own lives. Someone lives like Little Red Riding Hood, someone plays out the plot of the myth of Prometheus in their life and someone, like Hercules, atones for their sins by performing a series of significant feats.

As part of transactional analysis, the client has the opportunity to think about their own stories and scenarios. Perhaps it is not necessary for her chosen one to prove his love to her by risking his life in dangerous exploits, because she is not a princess in a tower guarded by a dragon. Scenario analysis could be very interesting if the therapist used tarot cards or some kind of oracle, such as Symbolon. In the cards, we rely on many myths and legends, and they correlate in an amazing way with the repertoire of our clients' psychological theatre. Here, the intersection of psychotherapy and tarot can lead to really deep and interesting work.

# SECTION 11. ESOTERIC ESSAY

## THE NARCISSISTIC ESOTERICISM OF MODERNITY

Engagement with esoteric subculture is often used as psychological compensation. And I must say that for narcissists, it is a very favourable environment. While in the ordinary sphere you need to make extensive efforts and grow professionally over a long period in order to flaunt your greatness, in modern esotericism everything can be done literally right away—if we are dealing with an extremely uneducated client who is not able to distinguish a professional from a charlatan.

Many practitioners revel in how magical and omnipotent they seem to people who, in a problematic and vulnerable state, come to them for help. The client does not understand and often does not want to understand how it all works. Once you start to understand the procedure, the feeling that it is a miracle will disappear, and with it that childish delight that so many want to preserve will vanish. Many practitioners embrace this. Rather than working with clarity, transparency and dialogue, they mystify, inflate and abundantly pin medals to their esoteric chest in order to be the most awesome and magically powerful magician or clairvoyant. And it works because we live in a society of social-media likes, fakes and simulacra, from which there is no escape.

It's clear with clients, but how do you keep yourself from slipping into malignant narcissism? And in general, how compatible is narcissism with the concept of spiritual growth?

There is an easy way to draw the line between healthy and malignant narcissism. Healthy narcissism involves loving yourself for something that is really present inside you. And moreover, this something benefits your own needs. That is, if a person wants to lead a good seminar, then he should do it, first of all, for himself because he likes the lesson and he will enjoy the process. But it often happens that a person needs to lead a seminar in order to prove something to someone, to impress colleagues or a mother, who in childhood constantly devalued their needs, and was proud only when they obediently went to a music school they hated. Healthy narcissists satisfy their own needs, while malignant narcissists have been accustomed, since childhood, to satisfying only the needs of those on whom they depend. They continue to do this even in adulthood, but they just cannot fill themselves in any way because their self-esteem is false, a leaky vessel that is constantly empty.

Therefore, while engaging in any esoteric practice, it is sensible to explore your fantasies. *Why am I doing this? How do I see my ideal professional image?* And here the imagination most often works as a traitor. *I want some special recognition. I would like not just to be listened to, but to be admired by those beneath me as a saviour. I want not to be ordinary, but to work miracles. And, of course, I want to have paranormal abilities, as they will certainly give me my long-awaited calm and power over others, the opportunity to prove once and for all that I am worth something.*

The trap is extremely dangerous. And the point is not that these fantasies need to be driven away. Rather, it must be realised that esotericism is not at all an assistant in their implementation. Narcissists, no matter what they say, need more than anything to accept their ordinariness. Esotericism can help them, but most often they come to this subculture for the wrong thing. Meditation, mindfulness, understanding how the world works, feeling like a small but important part of a larger plan—that's what could actually fill the void and help calm them down. But the malignant narcissist is more likely to choose magic and the ability to tailor the world to their needs.

So strong is their inner hunger that no other role than God suits them. But we often forget that to be God is to be invisible. The Higher Forces are not at all interested in public recognition, in adoration, in collecting stadiums of fans. They silently perform their task and do not attract attention to themselves. However, in the modern world of cinema and TV shows, even the Higher Forces are often presented in the form of gods who "wither and disappear" if people stop praying to and worshipping them. This is a tribute to the trends of the modern Western world.

In fact, a real mystic is well aware that the world has always existed and will continue to exist after this incarnation is completed. Accordingly, what is really omnipotent and eternal in them is not at all their earthly ego, which is subject to narcissism, but their Spirit, which, in fact, is not theirs at all, since at such a high level there is no longer a division into subject and object. There, the question of being better than anyone or competing with someone is simply inappropriate. Therefore, there is no such tendency towards narcissistic behaviour and compensation. The problem is that in order to hear your spiritual nature and join it, you need your very earthly ego to become light and transparent, and not overloaded with regalia and pomposity.

Loving yourself is good, but it is only possible to do this correctly if you have had experience of acceptance of your own characteristics and desires. If a person was not accepted and forced to be a narcissistic expansion of someone else, then they will use esotericism for exactly the same purpose, and, as with significant people in their childhood, they will never be able to get enough.

# SECTION 12. PROBLEMS OF THE TAROT COMMUNITY

## The Role of the Tarologist in the Client's Life

Of course, it would be better to ask clients about this, but not all of them would be able to formulate an answer, since they don't really think about this topic. Although, in my opinion, it would be nice for tarot readers to know exactly what function clients expect from them. I will not tire of repeating that the client comes to the tarot consultation very disoriented and in regression. The danger is that in this state the client will certainly mix contexts, which can greatly increase the psychological burden on tarologists.

The regressive state forces the client to delegate all of their needs to just one authority figure: the tarot reader, in this case. They become like a baby, for whom the mother represents the whole universe and must take care of their every need, from security to unconditional acceptance. A client with a problem can look at the tarologist with the same infantile, hopeful eyes hoping that we will take care of them. But the question is, what are the boundaries of our concern? What do we really need to do, and when should we help the client turn to someone else in their life?

To begin with, it must be established that we are not part of our client's family system. We are definitely not their mother, not their father, not their husband and not their wife. This entire series of books is built on the idea that clients will unconsciously bring transference reactions—unfinished patterns of previous relationships—to us for counselling. They will hope that we can finish the work that their relatives did not. But this is definitely not our task. I hope that after reading these four books, you will be able to recognise how and when a client brings these needs into the consultation. We should not indulge this behaviour because the format of tarot counselling will not allow us to really help the client in this matter. All we can do is recommend psychotherapy to them. Therapists really have the knowledge and the necessary tools to help the client in this matter. The purpose of you studying psychology is not at all in order to allow you to do this work instead of psychologists. But, as tarologists, we are often that intermediate link between the client and the psychotherapist, without which the client does not dare to turn to the right address.

The same is true of specialists in all other disciplines. We certainly cannot replace doctors, lawyers, notaries or financial advisors. This is a very important point. Despite the fact that questions to tarot cards can relate to absolutely any area of human life, we still should not do the work of other specialists. First, we do not have sufficient competence for this. Secondly, tarot cards provide information in a very specific way. It is not always possible to distinguish metaphorical meanings from direct ones. Some colleagues believe that cards work exclusively with a metaphorical level of information and do not provide any specifics at all.

What, then, is the tarologist's task? I propose to look at this question through the lens of comparison with a doctor. We go to the doctor when we have some kind of health problem or we want to go through a general medical examination and make sure that everything is in order. We do not ask the doctor about whether it is worth selling our apartment, whether it is worth going on vacation to a given country, or how relations with a loved one will develop. The competence of the doctor is very clearly defined. The doctor must not and cannot say anything that is not within their area of expertise. When it comes to esoteric consultation, we can describe everything in exactly the same way. During a consultation with a tarot reader, astrologer or other mantic, a client receives a "physical examination" only within the framework of the esoteric picture of the world, and nothing more.

A person can look into several different mirrors and see themselves slightly differently in each one. The same applies when it comes to different ways of considering themselves. For example, they will look into the psychological mirror and the mirror of medicine, and will not see any problems there. But they might look in the financial mirror and understand that their finances are not in the best condition now, and there is a threat. Esoteric discourse is useful only to those who already have elements of such a world view in their minds. If a person can see the world around them in the same way the esoteric sees it, then they will feel a need to know that everything is all right with them in this area, too.

A tarot consultant gives such a reflection. The consultant shows the client what they and their life look like in the reflection of an instrument of mystical quality. This does not mean that tarot cards cannot be laid out for a person who does not believe at all or rejects everything mystical. You can lay out the cards, you can get a completely adequate answer, but the client will not get any use out of this reflection, since they do not live in this world.

It may seem that I am suggesting that only questions of karma, hexes, destiny or the development of the soul can be viewed in the cards. No, I'm not saying that. You can ask any question, but it will be approached from an esoteric perspective. Tarot cards do not serve the earthly ego of a person; they work for a person's Higher Self. Therefore, buying a car may look good from a financial point of view, but not useful from an esoteric point of view. So, should the client buy a car? This is decided solely by the client, and no one else. But if the client comes to us, then they will be able to get an answer: how this purchase of a car looks not only from the point of view of ordinary earthly life but also from the point of view of higher plans. If the client cares at all about this, they will make a decision based on this information.

Tarot cards reflect a person and their life with esoteric discourse. If a person is interested in this perspective, then it is with us that they will receive it. This, in my opinion, is the unique role of a tarologist in the life of a client.

# PART THREE

# SECTION 1. ZODIAC

## Knight of Wands – Sagittarius

### *Upright Position*

Here is the third and last character of the suit of Wands, if we consider court cards according to the signs of the Zodiac. Like all figures of the suit of Fire, the Knight of Wands will also transmit an idealistic stream of energy, as did the Queen and King of Wands. But this time we are not dealing with just one, but with a whole multitude of different streams, which together can be combined into a whole philosophical or religious system. This might seem similar to the energy of the Queen and the King, but the difference here is colossal. The fact is that the Knight of Wands should not light up with an idea in order to transmit it, as the Queen of Wands does. He definitely does not need to identify with and get attached to the idea to be its viceroy on Earth, as the King of Wands does. The Knight of Wands is not at all dependent on the stream that he transmits, as he has a lot of these streams.

He is able to switch between them very easily. Today he talks about one value, tomorrow about another; the day after tomorrow he combines them both into a third. Let's not forget that he is still a representative of the element of Fire, which means that his ideas are still noble and sublime. He's not a prophet transmitting a revelation nor a priest with an entire church behind him; he is a spiritual teacher who can afford to slide between systems and offer each listener exactly the form of higher truth that will be most appropriate and helpful for them.

Such inner freedom from the energy stream also gives the Knight of Wands freedom from those who follow him. He will not defend these ideas if someone attacks or devalues them. He does not personally identify with the doctrine he preaches. For example, if he talks about some astrological truths, then he will not take any attacks on astrology personally. Astrology existed before him, and it will continue to exist after him. There is absolutely no need to protect it from anyone. It just doesn't need it. The same will be the case with any philosophical, religious or moral values that the Knight of Wands will speak about. They are transpersonal in nature and will always exist, no matter what an individual person thinks about them.

Later, we will compare this knight with other court card characters that we will discuss in the next books in the series. But now, we can give a small spoiler: two knights will always be responsible for the transmission of information and teaching—the Knight of Swords and the Knight of Wands. The first transmits information exclusively horizontally, like a regular school education or news bulletin—a quantitative accumulation of facts. Information of this kind is always impersonal. The second transmits information vertically, in which, along with the facts, values are also taught that transform the personality of the student. The Knight of Wands has an instinctive religiosity and philosophy from birth. Unlike the Knight of Pentacles, he does not need to prove that mystical worlds exist. The Knight of Wands acts as a spiritual teacher or medium who delivers personal spiritual messages or truths to a specific person.

Throughout these books, we will find four characters in whom we can definitely see signs of a neighbouring element, although they do not belong to it. The fiery Knight of Wands will have some signs of the element of Earth. The earthy Queen of Pentacles will have features of Air. The airy King of Swords will have characteristics of Water. And the watery Knight of Cups will have some signs of the Fire element. In the case of the Knight of Wands, we can say that he is translating or materialising subtle philosophical ideas into earthly forms. He forms values into a doctrine or philosophy so that they can be passed on, disseminated and left to posterity. This is also the main characteristic of the King of Pentacles, but he will not be so focused on values and philosophy but more on art and beauty. So, the Knight of Wands is a unique teacher who will explain the theory of relativity to one person through formulas, to another with his fingers, and to a third through Lego bricks.

Of course, not every Knight of Wands will necessarily be a highly spiritual person. In the usual worldly version, we will get an inexhaustible optimist and a cheerful person who has to use the inner fire in order to dispel any hopelessness. Such people are attracted to holidays, parties, pleasures. He is the older brother who takes his younger brother out into the world. And he will not only be able to protect him from some dangers but also teach him everything he needs to know for a comfortable life in this world. This is a friend who will forcefully drag you out of the house to a party if you are moping and do not want to go anywhere. This is a child who comes to a tired parent in the evening and asks to play with them, making the parent change their mood; they start smiling and forget about their adult difficulties and worries.

Whoever the Knight of Wands is, we will receive from him an expansion of opportunities, a surge of positive energy, as well as a rise in optimism. This is vitality in its purest form, which many people can temporarily lose when they encounter difficulties in their own lives.

*Reversed Position*

As with any reversed card, we get some glitches in the settings. With regard to the reversed Knight of Wands, we can say that he sees "heaven" very well, but sees "earth" very poorly. He loses the ability to choose the right words to convey his truths and values to a particular person. The reversed Knight of Wands is focused on his ideas to the detriment of reality, which is why his teaching becomes fanatical, and he turns into a Black Teacher, who harms and destroys rather than raises a person's level of development.

Such failures in the settings can manifest in several ways. First is the classic pearls being cast before swine. The reversed Knight of Wands may have the right idea, but may not find the right time and place to preach it. He ceases to feel the needs of the people who came to listen to him. As a result, he does not hit the target at all. In the second version, the reversed Knight of Wands correctly finds the addressee, but his form of presenting the truth is greatly distorted. He still can't find the right words and starts to sound like a fanatic. Now he will definitely begin to defend his teaching, which he would never do with the upright position of the card. He will forcibly make you a saint, although you did not ask him about it at all.

The promises of the reversed Knight of Wands become absolutely unreliable. It is important to note here that this has nothing to do with lying or being manipulative, it's just that such a Knight lives only in the world of ideas. It seems to him that the promise of help is already help. He forgets that this help still needs to be implemented in the real world to transfer it from the element of fire to the element of earth. This he usually forgets to do, and then he will be sincerely surprised and offended when he is accused of inconsistency.

In the reversed position, the stream of the Knight of Wands also narrows, as is the case with the Queen and King of Wands. His ideas and values become superficial and profane. One gets the feeling that he himself does not grasp the deep essence of what he is talking about. But the reversed Knight of Wands will certainly say all these things with the pathos of a preacher, which will make him seem ridiculous and stupid. The reversed court cards of the suit of Fire are always distinguished by some arrogance, and the Knight of Wands will not be an exception to this rule at all.

The superficiality of the reversed Knight of Wands is also reflected in his complete irresponsibility towards others. In the example above, it would look like this: the older brother will take his inexperienced younger brother into the big outside world and forget him somewhere, lose him, because he will be carried away by something extraneous. Or, instead of giving him useful advice on how to live in the adult world, he will teach his little brother something really bad and harmful. In the example with a friend: he will promise that at the party you will unwind and perk up, and once you're there, he will immediately switch to some acquaintances he has not seen for ages and leave you. And you will stand among all these people dancing and having fun, and feel as if you are a fish that was washed ashore by a wave.

The reversed Knight of Wands has another very unpleasant quality—this is his exorbitant boasting. It usually looks like this: you start talking about the fact that you have some kind of object, or you have been somewhere, or you know how to do something. The reversed Knight of Wands will immediately begin to convince you that he also has the same object, that he visited this place last year and that his grandmother taught him this skill when he was a child. At first, you will believe him, but then you will begin to understand that the numbers in this whole equation simply do not converge. You'll see him doing exactly the same trick with another person in your presence and know he is definitely lying. For the reversed Knight of Wands, it is simply unbearable to admit that he doesn't have something, that he hasn't been somewhere, or that he doesn't know how to do something.

The complacency of the reversed Knight of Wands is truly enormous. And since he still belongs to the suit of Fire, his energy stream and pressure are above average in strength. When he talks about a topic, it may seem that he really understands it. He knows and uses technical terms, pretends to be smart, talks about some books. But we must remember that this is dust in the eyes, designed for those who know nothing about this topic. As soon as he says the same thing in the presence of a real expert, it costs nothing to expose him. In fact, he has always just been talking nonsense, but he does it with a smart look and uses words that neither you nor he know the meaning of.

Thus, the reversed Knight of Wands pursues prestige. Here, he begins to look a little like the reversed King of Wands, who invests in creating a magnificent facade to hide his inner emptiness. The reversed Knight of Wands has serious doubts about his own intellect, so he compensates with an external mask of false expertise.

# SECTION 2. VIGNETTE

## EMPRESS TAKES OFF HER CROWN, CHAPTER 5

Emma didn't have a particularly busy day today, with just three clients booked. She'd agreed to meet with John later. Liz was right; there was something about this guy that attracted her. She'd called him the day after their first unsuccessful meeting and offered to meet again for a cup of coffee. She wanted to rehabilitate herself after her narcissistic outburst the first time. At the second meeting, she made sure to ask him questions about himself and quickly realised that he had completely destroyed all her stereotypes about physical education teachers and fitness coaches.

John was her age, had a higher sports education and had had a good career in the past as a professional gymnast. But the careers of athletes are quite short, so soon enough he'd had to leave professional sports. He said that he'd been worried, as his daily routine had changed a lot. He'd decided "not to sit at home and turn blue", but to go to university. In the end, he graduated with a master's degree, and since then had had two jobs, one "for the soul" and the second "for the money". He wasn't the coach of the school sports team—his colleague took care of that. He worked with the children at school just for fun. But in the gym he worked with private clients, and they paid him well.

In appearance, John really looked like a typical athlete—a very good and strong body. However, he was not at all obsessed with his appearance. He dressed casually, but he looked good and very attractive. Emma had at first been worried that he would be dumb, but it turned out that John was just as well-read as Tom. He was interested in philosophies of health but was no fanatic. "I just want to understand more deeply what the body is and how we are arranged," he'd told her.

It was interesting with him. And he seemed absolutely simple, which was captivating for Emma. She relaxed very quickly next to him. He fit in perfectly with Tom and Liz, as he had similar interests, and by nature he was not trying to impress anyone. John and Emma had been meeting for several months since the summer, and an affair had begun between them. Emma was really happy with everything. John was the perfect man for her in every way, although he didn't look like it at first. Emma certainly wasn't going to introduce him to her parents, at least not yet, since her father wouldn't like him. John had no inclination to fawn over anyone, and Emma's father was best not approached without the ritual of five prostrations. She also preferred not to tell her esoteric friends about John, as she understood how they were from different planets. That is, Emma began to zealously defend their relationship from the outside world, since it seemed to her that it could somehow stain the naturalness and ease between them.

The doorbell rang and Emma went to meet her last client for the day. When she opened the door, at first it seemed to her that something was wrong with her eyesight. The sensation was such that a strong beam of a spotlight had hit her in the face, like on a stage or at a disco. In front of her stood a young (most likely) girl, dressed in a bright pink fur coat and snow-white short trousers. The purse on the client's shoulder was covered with rhinestones, which made it shine like a disco ball.

"Hiiiii there!" the girl drawled in an unnatural, childish tone. At the same time, her body somehow arched unnaturally, as if she was posing for a selfie.

Emma greeted and invited the client in.

"I'm Susie!" said the girl. Her intonation on the two syllables of her name managed to jump up and down five times. High heels thumped on the floor of the corridor as if she was still trying to dance. Susie did not take off her fur coat, and entered the room, sitting in a client chair.

Now Emma was able to get a better look at her. It became clear what had confused her at first. It was not even so much the clothes and voice of the client—it was that she seemed to have been completely reshaped from head to toe by a plastic surgeon. Definitely lips, nose, breasts, perhaps ears—all this has been "improved". The girl was wearing a whole ton of makeup, obnoxiously bright and obviously unnecessary. Aggressively red nails and lips, about seven or eight rings on her fingers that jingled against each other while she theatrically sat down in the chair and straightened her hair. The whole image looked so unnatural that it was difficult for Emma to tell how old the client really was. She definitely wanted to look eighteen, although she looked at least twice that.

Emma felt embarrassed that she was staring at Susie so closely.

"I'm already thirty-eight years old," lisped Susie, as if offended, "and all my relationships keep falling apart! Maybe we'll look at the cards and see, well, what, what, what's wrong with me!"

Emma couldn't take her eyes off Susie. The client aroused strange feelings. Emma was about to burst into laughter. It felt like she was watching a hilarious comedy with very talented actors and a great script. But she pulled herself together. The question was serious, and she should certainly never laugh at the client.

Emma picked up a deck of cards and asked, "Are you dating anyone now?"

"Yes." Susie winked conspiratorially. "I'll tell you now."

From her shiny purse she took out a pink notebook with cats on the cover and a pink feather for a bookmark, which immediately smelled of a generous portion of perfume, and began to leaf through it.

"Can we check about a few guys?"

"Yes, we can," Emma agreed.

This was not such a rare issue. Quite often, clients wanted to analyse the topic of relationships and compare potential partners. The cards always gave a good and deep analysis and helped the client begin to understand what was happening in their sphere of feelings and what they might not have noticed about the relationship.

"Do I need to tell you the name?" Susie asked.

"Not necessarily, just think of the person you would like to ask about. I'll just ask you one thing before we start. What would you like ideally from a relationship? What are you striving for?"

"I want to get married!" Susie pouted her lips even more. "But somehow, I can't. I can't find a decent man."

"I understand," Emma said. "Think of the first man."

"Done." Susie nodded. "I'll still say the names, otherwise I will get myself confused. This will be Nick."

Emma dealt the first spread to understand where she should start interpreting.

"Isn't he married?" Emma asked when she saw the Ten of Pentacles, which in tarot, among other things, denoted family unions.

"Oh, yes!" Susie agreed. "To this frump. You should have seen her!"

"Sorry to upset you," said Emma, "but he is unlikely to leave the family. I don't know what he is telling you, but it is clear that he is firmly present in the family. There must be children there. And there are strong financial ties. He couldn't just leave, even if he really wanted to. And in general, he looks like he does not consider you an adult. And he seems to me to be a little tough and rude."

Susie listened and nodded, her mouth slightly open. It seemed that this information did not surprise or upset her at all. She quickly scribbled a couple of lines in her notebook and immediately suggested the next name.

"And if we try Patrick?" she asked.

Emma collected the cards, shuffled them, and dealt another spread.

"There are a lot of sexual cards in here," Emma said.

"Oh yeah..." Susie said pointedly. "You have no idea!"

"But I don't see much pleasure here either, just as I don't see the desire to create a union. And that reversed Magician at the top hints that he uses you. Have you noticed this?"

Susie winced. It was evident that the topic of sex caused her some mixed feelings. On the one hand, she looked like an advertisement for a sex shop, but on the other, there was a feeling that she herself did not want to have anything to do with what she was advertising.

"He knows how to be so generous," she said. "These are the shoes he bought me, by the way." She took off her shoe and practically handed it to Emma.

Emma gestured for her to take away her shoe. Susie put her shoe back on and began to list all the things that this man had given her. According to her, he was a "Honey Bear", so strong and gentle. He loved her so much and cherished her so much.

"And where does this... guy work?" Emma almost said "Honey Bear".

"He's with a security firm," Susie said. "He's so strong. I've never seen such huge muscles. When he hugs me, I feel like I'll suffocate with excitement."

Emma was sure that the list would not end with Patrick. And sure enough, more and more guys followed. Emma was already confused about their names. The cards nevertheless showed the same steady trend. In all spreads there were reversed Kings or other symbols denoting tough and unpleasant men, as well as a lot of cards that represented childhood. Not a single card that could be interpreted as a stable emotional attachment. Not a hint of marriage, or at least of serious intentions.

"You keep getting the same male type here," Emma said. "All these men are tough, and I would even say that they are cold and insensitive. This is what abusers and criminals often look like. Not that I'm implying that you're messing with lawbreakers. But I see a lot of strength here and at the same time either a lack of experience with or an inability to have a full family life. Tell me, could you describe to me what your ideal man is?"

Susie really liked this question. It was like a little girl was asking another little girl to make a unicorn collage. She smacked her lips sweetly, leaned back in her chair, and her tone became even more childish and unnatural. Emma felt like she was at a primary-school show.

Susie's ideal man, she said, should be rich, preferably at least fifty years old, with a big house and several cars. He should also have his own business, preferably a large one. He must be very athletic and strong.

"What about his family experience?" Emma asked. "By the age of fifty, a man should definitely have at least some family or relationship experience."

"It doesn't matter," said Susie. "By the age of fifty, married women are usually terrible. Let her be hidden away somewhere in one of his mansions—she can get her maintenance money, so long as she does not get in my way."

Emma was a little taken aback. She had an idea of what businessmen were like. Yes, some of them had mistresses, but she also knew that under no circumstances could these lovers replace the wife. These men were always family men, and they came to all events with their wives. Mistresses were part of some shady and secret other life. Yes, they were taken on vacation, they were bought expensive gifts, but these men definitely did not consider their lovers to be someone serious. Emma would've felt sorry for such women, if not for one thing: many of them had such high opinions of themselves, as if they really were in a high position. As if being someone's lover automatically made them very important.

"You know," said Emma, "so far, all the men you've asked about do not fit your goals. I also cannot say that I have seen a tendency to part in any of these spreads. All these men may continue to be present in your life, as they are now, but they are unlikely to give you what you need. Tell me, do you work?"

"I've got a YouTube channel," Susie said proudly. "Sometimes you can earn something. But I believe that I should not work for survival. I can fully devote myself to my man, and let him provide for me. It's not a woman's destiny to work. Work disfigures and ages women. I must always be beautiful, fresh and full of energy. A man should look at me and get inspired. Although, that is also work. Do you know how much effort and time it takes to look like this?"

"I can imagine." Emma felt herself starting to get annoyed with this client. She had heard that, even in esotericism, there was a whole movement that inspired women towards such an infantile model of behaviour. If she remembered correctly, it was called Vedic philosophy, though it had nothing to do with the Vedas. But courses of this kind sold well. Women there were made into brainless dolls who had to wear only dresses, forget about their own careers and sense of worth and dignity, and only look for a man to completely depend on. This was so contrary to Emma's values that she felt disgust for the leaders of such courses, and, for their victims, a certain pity and sympathy.

"Do your girlfriends have long-term relationships? Are they married?" Emma asked, thinking that the client might simply lack the right example in her life.

"I don't have many friends," Susie said. "Oh, can you check one more man?"

Emma began shuffling the deck of cards again. The spread came out a little different, and Emma was a little surprised by this change in the picture.

"Look—this is a completely different option," she said. "A guy with a normal character, hardworking, honest and conscientious.

Not quite what you would like for the money, but it may be that he just has a seasonal job. He could make a lot of money, too. Can't figure out if he's free..."

"That's my coach at the gym," Susie said with slight disdain in her voice. "Gorgeous body, but what money is there?"

"What's his name?" Emma asked tensely, but then she came to her senses. Why did she ask? She'd said herself that names were not important.

"Steve," Susie replied. "But he's also kind of unfree."

"What do you mean 'kind of'?"

"Well, he's married." Susie grimaced. "To this Stacy, who is the administrator at the counter and teaches yoga classes in the evening. Scary cow! I don't understand what he sees in her." She began to speak in a vile whisper, leaning slightly forward. "If I only wanted to, he would be mine in three minutes. I see how he smiles at me, how he flirts and winks."

"Oh, God..." Emma could not stand it, abruptly putting the cards aside.

Susie broke off and looked fearfully at the tarot reader.

"Don't you hear yourself?" Emma said irritably. "Maybe with her, with this 'scary cow', he has exactly the relationship that you dream of getting?"

Susie turned pale, and all her theatricality and childish playfulness completely disappeared.

Emma was scared for some reason. She couldn't remember the last time she'd felt such intense and concentrated fear. She felt like a mother who'd slapped her daughter and miscalculated her strength. It seemed that Susie was choosing what was best: to fight this woman with the cards, or release the tears of resentment that were beginning to choke her from the inside.

She decided to defend herself.

"I won't stoop that low! He's dirt broke. I'm worth a lot more, in case you haven't noticed. I don't understand what makes you so angry?"

Emma realised that she had gone too far. This doll sitting opposite her was very annoying, but Emma had allowed herself to speak her mind too much. Her task was to interpret the cards, not to give out moralising lectures.

The fear went away, but she became embarrassed and ashamed, and she tried to save the situation.

"Sorry, that may have sounded rude. I certainly did not mean to say that you are unworthy of something. I just can't help but see the contradiction. You said that you are thirty-eight, but you are not in a relationship yet. That is, there is no relationship that would suit you. You are a bright woman; men pay attention to you. Maybe you just pay attention to the wrong men? Maybe if you change your search criteria a little, everything will work out?"

Susie began to recover. Her facial features softened a little. Emma relaxed a bit too. Certainly, the client did not look vindictive.

"Well, I don't know," Susie replied. "Sometimes I think I'm just not meant to be happy. Maybe someone cursed me? Can you check?"

Emma was glad for a change of subject. Although she knew the answer to the client's question even without the cards.

She drew the Six of Cups from the deck.

"There is no curse here—not even close. Look, the card shows a couple. Plus, it is very bright and kind. But it does not suggest development. This represents nostalgia for the past, not a desire to move into the future. And this shows a circle of people that is already narrow to you. You need to find a new circle of friends."

Susie looked unhappy with this interpretation. She pursed her lips in resentment and turned to the window.

"Did I upset you?" Emma asked.

"No, no." The client shook her head. "But I have a feeling that you don't like me, or you don't understand what I'm talking about.

But okay, it doesn't matter. I've already received the answers to my questions. Thank you."

"Sorry again," Emma said.

On the one hand, she felt she had ruined the consultation. On the other hand, she was glad that the client was leaving and not asking Emma to deny that she didn't like her. She really didn't like her very much.

"May everything turn out the way you want it to," Emma said, seeing Susie off. "I certainly didn't mean to offend you."

# SECTION 3. CHARACTEROLOGY

## The Histrionic Character

### Childhood

"Histrionic" is a modern term, although it should be noted that in Freud's time this character was called "hysterical" and was extremely widespread in bourgeois society. In fact, Freud formulated many of the theories that later formed the basis of psychoanalysis while working with this type of patient. It is believed to occur much more frequently in women. So it was in the 19th century, and so it is now. Meeting a histrionic man is much rarer than meeting a histrionic woman, and we will now figure out the reason.

Experts most often describe two family scenarios that greatly contribute to the development of a histrionic character. In the first scenario, there is a markedly unequal attitude towards the male and female sexes in the family. Any manifestations of masculinity are welcomed and encouraged as much as possible, and feminine features are denied and devalued. If a girl grows up in such a family, then the father will only notice her outward signs of femininity, and he will ignore her emotionality. It is very difficult for a girl to please such a father. If she has a brother, then she constantly sees how her father punishes or ridicules him for any manifestations of gentleness and sensitivity. "Why are you crying like a girl?" her father will shout at her brother, and the girl understands that her sensuality, softness and subtlety do not attract her father at all. He constantly makes it clear that neither he nor the world around him needs these qualities. Only masculinity, strength, perseverance and insensitivity have real meaning and value.

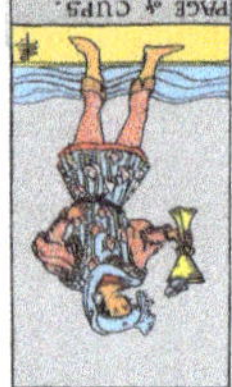

Even in childhood, the girl is clearly made to understand that she is a second-class creature. She was not lucky enough to be born a boy. Her father loves and appreciates her brother much more, even if he is much less talented than her. At the same time, the girl begins to notice the power of female sexuality over a man. She sees how this formidable and strong man softens, and melts, becoming complaisant and obedient when there's a seductive and beautiful woman in front of him. At this moment, a tragedy happens in the child's psyche, which will then launch the development of a histrionic character. The girl begins to use her own sexuality in order to receive acceptance and protection from the man. The problem is that she just ends up being sexually exploited and never getting what she needs. Children's sexuality has nothing to do with adult sexuality. The child simply wants admiration and acceptance, wants it in that naive manner that the child's psyche is capable of. The child definitely does not want a real sexual relationship. The mechanism that develops in the histrionic personality is sad precisely because the person wants love and acceptance in a naive and pure manner but uses adult sexual seduction for this.

A mother in such a family also does not make life easier for her daughter. When a girl ridiculously and theatrically tries to "seduce" her father, since it is very important for her to win his attention and see admiration in his eyes, the mother begins to punish her daughter as if she were not a child but a real adult rival trying to take away her man. The mother becomes cold, rejecting and shaming. Sometimes she openly takes out her own anger and sexual frustration on her daughter. In psychological literature, one can often find descriptions of the envy of an ageing mother (who is losing her attractiveness) for the youth and fertility of her daughter. Such a mother is capable of causing great harm to her daughter. The psychological influence and power of a mother over the psyche of her child should by no means be underestimated. Even in adulthood, the words of a mother can hurt much more than the words of any other person. If the mother is jealous of the child, she is able to do quite a lot of damage to the child's self-esteem.

In such a situation, the girl experiences the second betrayal. One role of the mother is to help the daughter through female initiation, to help her understand how to live in a female body, how to properly care for it. The child initially does not know anything about this; she needs to be taught all these things. A girl who later develops a histrionic character is rejected by both parents. The father sees in her only external beauty but does not recognise her inner femininity as valuable. And the mother sees in her a competitor and punishes the child for manifestations of the same femininity. In this case, the feminine nature of the girl cannot fully develop. It acquires pretentious and theatrical features, remaining inside quite infantile in essence. She becomes a woman, with the most emphasised attributes of femininity, who remains a weak and vulnerable child inside.

The second family scenario is always associated with the concept of incest. Immediately, it is necessary to make the reservation that we are not necessarily talking about sexual harassment of a child, although this is not excluded. However, such a crime is more likely to lead to the development of a dissociative character, which we will talk about in the third book of the series.

This is about metaphorical seduction. Parents in such a family might walk around naked in the apartment in front of the child. Perhaps some erotic or pornographic materials are in the common areas, or the child often becomes an unwitting witness to the sexual relations of adults. At such moments, the child's psyche is overexcited. It is incapable of processing and coping with such a complex phenomenon as adult sexuality. There are also genuinely incestuous scenarios when the father does not respect the intimate bodily space of the child. He may not put an adult sexual meaning into it, but the child is overexcited when she is touched where she is not supposed to be, when she is tickled, so she starts laughing hysterically and the adult does not want to stop. Some experts also include in this category cases when one of the parents sleeps in the same bed with the child for longer than expected, while the second sleeps in another room. In infancy and early childhood, this is acceptable, but then it leads to negative consequences.

The most important conclusion we need to make about the histrionic character is that the child chooses the adult sexual seduction strategy in order to gain acceptance, protection and admiration. Sexuality in such a person remains childish, so in adulthood this leads to big problems in building romantic and sexual relationships. The partner is often unwittingly deceived. The histrionic character approaches like a sexually sophisticated adult, the partner is seduced by such an unambiguous proposal, and then it turns out that he is facing a defenceless child who has been molested. In such a situation, both partners suffer, although everything is not always so obvious.

## Adulthood

An adult histrionic character is always characterised by great theatricality and brightness in their mannerisms. It seems that they are constantly trying to impress, please and seduce. They are very concerned about their appearance, very afraid of ageing, and act like they are on stage. Only, unlike the narcissists, for them this is not a podium or a pulpit, it is rather a pole in a strip club. Seduction always has a strong sexual connotation.

It is important to note that histrionic characters sometimes do not even realise how much seduction is in their behaviour. Such people sincerely wonder why others constantly react to them sexually because they do not mean to be perceived that way. Their messages, in fact, are very difficult to read in a non-sexual way, given all their theatricality and emphasis. But the histrionic character is very afraid of being sexually exploited. It is a repetition of their past trauma. In addition, they are deeply convinced that love and acceptance must be paid for with sex, and such a reaction from adults only confirms for them this wrong attitude.

Histrionic women very often choose "daddies" as partners. Usually, these are men who are really more suitable for such women as fathers, but in the eyes of a histrionic woman, they possess all those enviable trappings of masculinity that she so desperately seeks. In her picture of the world, femininity is still second-rate, and only masculinity has real value. Moreover, her infantile character is still looking for a parent, as it tries to receive what it lacked in childhood—protection, acceptance and admiration. Unfortunately, these relationships often turn out to be dead ends for two reasons. First, the sphere of big business and politics, where the histrionic woman is looking for such men, is not a sphere of soft and tender teddy bears, but a pool of toothy sharks. To survive and achieve success in these areas, you need to be tough and cold. The histrionic character cannot distinguish between force and cruelty. Therefore, in a relationship, she chooses either narcissists or sociopaths. The first are simply not able to admire someone other than themselves, and the latter are completely devoid of empathy and prone to real cruelty. It's definitely impossible to get love, care and admiration from such men. The second reason is that even if the "daddy" turns out to be caring, he will not let such a woman grow up and become an adult. In the second book, we will talk in detail about the topic of the oral character. Such a partner will provide sacrificial care, and at first the histrionic woman will be happy. But he won't let her grow up and mature. Her sexuality will remain childlike. And in the end, she herself will devalue the gentleness and care of such a man, considering him to be not masculine enough, and therefore, not valuable.

Another feature of the histrionic character is simply a pathological craving for love triangles. A non-free man seems more attractive than a free one. The psyche again tries to complete what did not work out in childhood. In this case, this is competition with the mother. In such a relationship, there is always a haunting ghost in the form of another woman or wife. It is curious that without her, the histrionic character often loses interest in this man. He is valuable as long as he chooses a lover and not a wife. Such women can live in this pattern for years without even knowing they are being sexually exploited. Despite the fact that this man may constantly promise that he will leave his wife, divorce her and stay forever with his young lover, he will never do this. Or he will definitely "do it tomorrow", but that "tomorrow" never comes. In connection with this pattern of behaviour, it is necessary to mention the Oedipus complex, but we will talk about this in more detail in the following sections.

Relationships with other women often develop in strange ways. There is a fairly close but dependent relationship with the mother, who continues to actively interfere in her daughter's adult life. There may be girlfriends, but they, as a rule, also have a strong histrionic character radical. When they hang out together, they act like little girls. They get together, lisp, go shopping, buy clothes, go to beauty salons, but secretly hate each other and dream about how they will meet that very strong man. In such friendship groups there is no real emotional acceptance or adult contact. It's like a game, and it remains a game when it comes to providing real help for each other's problems. Children cannot help.

### Need

The histrionic woman does not feel valued. She sincerely believes that value can only be acquired through contact with a strong man. Analysts often write that sex for such women is often unconsciously associated with some kind of magical ritual, during which a man endows a woman with his power. In fact, these sexual relationships only help her for a while, as stable relationships are never created.

It is necessary for a histrionic character to receive admiration and care from a strong, adult man without paying for this with sexuality. The magic happens when such a man really treats such a woman with warmth and care and, despite her desperate attempts to seduce him, gently refuses her without devaluing her sexuality. A woman can also give a histrionic character an experience of acceptance without competition. She can set an example of what adult femininity and sexuality are, in order to show that both sexes can be strong and valuable and give the histrionic character a positive version of femininity to appropriate.

# SECTION 4. CORE TERM

## TRIANGULATION

From the name itself, it should be obvious that this term has something to do with triangles. But what these triangles are is not entirely clear. Before we begin, I want to say that this topic, as far as I know, has never been covered in the literature on tarot cards, although it is directly related to tarot counselling.

There is a point of view, and in my opinion a quite fair one, that in infancy a child does not perceive anyone at all except for his mother. At this stage, the child does not even perceive his mother as a separate entity. The psyches of the mother and the infant are merged, and only later, towards the end of the first year, when the child learns to crawl, will the first separation crisis occur. The child will understand that, in addition to the mother, there is a huge world, and exploratory activity will wake up in them. The father, as such, may be present in the world of the baby, but it is unlikely that the child at this age distinguishes these two parental figures as heterosexual. The child does not yet realise that they have a certain gender themselves. Identification with gender and with one of the parents will occur later. So far, we have a stable dyad "child–mother", and at this stage they do not need anyone else.

Triangulation is the process by which a dyad becomes a triad, or a pair becomes a triangle. This is an absolutely natural stage of development, which takes place in childhood, when the child begins to notice the father. Within the framework of family psychology, triangulation also happens to adults when a child appears in their family. There were two of them, and now there are three of them. Such a process always entails a significant restructuring of roles. All functions must be redistributed in a new way. This is considered a crisis moment, since these are not only quantitative but also qualitative changes. Not only are there more participants in the relationship, they now perform completely new functions. There are quite a few such triangulation processes in life at various stages of human development and in various areas: relationships, work and even methodology (more on that at the very end).

Most often, triangulation is a natural requirement in the logical development of a couple. When the couple has exhausted its resources, it is obliged to expand to three. Problems occur when triangulation happens much earlier than the situation requires. It would be better to give a few examples here.

Classical triangulation is the creation of a love triangle. Where there was a couple, a third person appears. And in this case, this triangulation does not help the couple to develop qualitatively. This third person is wedged into contact with them and draws some of the energy of the couple. In the previous section, we considered the histrionic character and talked about the fact that such women prefer to initially establish relationships with already married men. That is, they triangulate the relationship of such a man, creating an additional pole. And they themselves are trying to live correctly the failed triangulation of their childhood, when the Oedipus complex (competition with the parent of the same sex for the parent of the opposite sex) was not experienced correctly. A histrionic character cannot simply be in a couple. It's boring and uninteresting. It is much more exciting to participate in hidden competition.

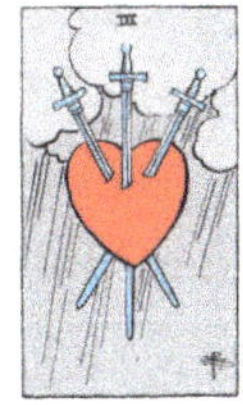

There are quite a few examples of such triangles in psychology. In the last book in this series, in the section on addictions, we will discuss the famous Karpman triangle, which is very common in addictive families. "Victim–Rescuer–Persecutor": these are the roles that must be present so that such a family can continue to function. There are also triads such as "Child–Parent–Adult", which we considered in the framework of Transactional Analysis.

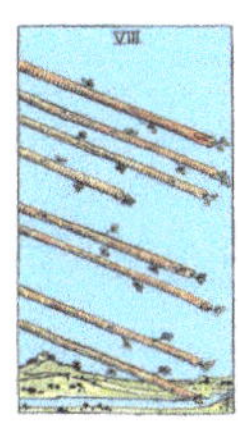

It is important for us to understand the following: triangulation should be a natural part of a couple's development, not a way to avoid complications within the couple. Finding a third person is often easier because the third draws onto themselves the tension within the couple but at the same time does not allow the couple to clarify the complexity that has appeared and move forward.

What does this have to do with tarot counselling? I am sure everyone would agree that tarot consultation is a dyadic process. There is a tarot reader and there is a client (unless, of course, we personify the cards and consider the consultation as a séance at which the Higher Forces are present). The fact is that clients very often cannot stay in the dyad, and begin to triangulate the relationship. The client might draw the tarot reader into a relationship from the client's life, creating a triangle. For example, triangulation occurs when a husband comes for a consultation, and after a while his wife comes for her own consultation. Or the daughter comes for a reading, and a short time later, so does her mother. But she doesn't tell the tarot reader that she's the mother of the client he worked with last week. She asks the same questions as her daughter, hoping for one of two things. On the one hand, she might want to check for herself what the "cards say" and get exactly the opposite opinion that her daughter did. That is, she draws the tarologist into her conflict with her daughter, making them the third wheel in their pair. On the other hand, the mother may be spying on her daughter. I have had such cases. She hopes that the tarot reader will not respect the rules of confidentiality and will tell her what they told her daughter, and even better, what the daughter herself asked.

Clients love to involve a specialist in their family disputes so much that psychologists, for example, have clear rules in this regard: they will not communicate with anyone from their client's life, they will only communicate with the client during consultations, and they will not allow triangulation context or to be involved in a friendship, sexual relationship or other collaboration with the client. In the realm of tarot, there are no restrictions on working with only one relative and not interacting with their loved ones. Maybe this rule will someday appear, since psychologists introduced it for their own safety.

Triangulation can also be used as a method by tarologists. Today, you can often encounter a situation where a specialist uses more than one method in their work. For example, they may simultaneously look at the client's question using the tarot deck and some kind of oracle. They may involve two mantic systems in their consultation, for example: tarot and astrology. These are examples of useful triangulation, when the techniques begin to complement and correct each other.

The client most often resorts to triangulation unconsciously. But we, as consultants, must see when it is important to remain in the dyad, and when it is more appropriate to rely on the triad. Sometimes we have to deny a client a triad, even if they insist on it. They do not always realise that this can create problems not only for them but also for the tarologist.

# SECTION 5. THEORETICAL LECTURE

## SEXOLOGY

I would like to begin this section with a serious warning. It is difficult to find a more intriguing and attractive topic than sexuality. It is mercilessly exploited today by almost everyone who can. Whether it's in cinema, literature, advertising or some other area, certain elements of eroticism attract the viewer and the buyer. In psychological or other counselling services, things are very similar. If a particular training course is about sexuality, it will attract more students than anything else. And, of course, in this topic we will observe the most ethical violations. It varies from country to country as to whether you need a license to call yourself a psychologist or sexologist, but people should be especially cautious when they agree to counselling or training in the field of sexology. This is a separate and extremely complex sphere of knowledge that requires training no less serious than other professions. You can't just read a few sexology books or take a year-long course to declare yourself a sexologist. Clients should always check what training and work experience such a "supposed specialist" has.

For tarologists, I would like to make a separate warning. Today, there are a large number of erotic and sexual tarot decks. Special books have been written for them. But these are books on tarot, not sexology. You can't just pick up an erotic deck and immediately become an expert in such a complex topic. Moreover, issues of sexuality require the practitioner to be especially subtle and tactful in their work. Talking about the client's sex life is not the same as discussing a career or buying a car. With this topic, we enter a secret and intimate zone and we are obliged to work with the utmost care. Moreover, if the client does not personally raise this topic, there is definitely no need to forcefully pull them there. Of course, which deck to work with is the personal choice of the tarot reader, but in my experience, erotic decks can significantly distort and sexualise the process. The client is distracted by these images and is often unable to focus on anything but the sexual topic. This was something I realised during my research based on different decks. As a result, erotic-themed decks had to be excluded from the study, as they worked like an artefact and greatly distorted the results. It will be better if you work with a classic deck or a deck made in a slightly different style.

Like any other field, sexology contains a huge number of interesting topics. We could talk about the physiology and formation of sexual behaviour, or various addictions or disorders of sexual desire. Separately, there are issues of gender identity and sexual orientation. But within the framework of this series of books we will focus on just one topic: the stages of psychosexual development. If the reader is interested in this area, they can additionally find a lot of high-quality professional literature on this subject.

Perhaps we need to start with the most important thing and remind the reader that human sexuality is by no means limited to the sexual act alone. Everything is much more complicated. It all starts in early childhood when the child experiences an emotional attraction to their own parents and later to peers. Here, in no case is it necessary to consider children's sexuality from the perspective of an adult. This is by no means incest or any deviation. All a child wants is emotional connection and acceptance. He wants to please certain people, admire them, attract attention and exchange feelings.

Speaking about the stages of psychosexual development, one should start from the age of about 10–12 years, when the so-called platonic stage begins in the future teenager. Here, everything revolves around the child's fantasy of the chosen person. They begin to dream of spending time together, of sharing feelings. There is no hint of adult sexuality here. He just wants to be looked at. He would like to present a toy to his friend. He would like to invite this particular girl to his birthday. He wants her to talk to him and not to anyone else. It would seem that everything is so childishly innocent and frivolous—Where is the sexuality here?—but this stage is very important in the development of the child and the future adult. The ability to fantasise and dream about a loved one creates the most important psychological basis for building further relationships. Everyone fell in love as a child and can remember how they behaved at that age. I mention this experience because it is very important later in a person's development.

Then, at the age of about 12–16 years, the second stage begins, which in the literature is called the erotic stage. Here, the contents of fantasies change somewhat. "Now I don't just want to spend time together, I want some tactile sensations." In particular, touching, kissing and hugging become especially important. Now it is important not just to walk together, but to hold hands at the same time. Fantasies at first are not at all about sex, but for now only about the nakedness of a partner. And only then comes the actual sexual stage, at which sexual relations begin in the adult understanding of this concept.

In adulthood, everything should happen in exactly the same way as in childhood, only in a shorter time frame. That is, everything should begin simply with falling in love, when a potential partner stands out from the environment and the mind is filled with platonic fantasies about time spent together. Then the couple should be at the erotic stage for some time, enjoy touching, hugging and kissing, and only then should they move on to sexual relations. But this is in the textbook. In life, especially in modern times, things are somewhat different. Many couples, literally from the first meeting, fly straight into a sexual relationship. That is, they start with sex, and only then try to build a romantic foundation for a future relationship. But it is very difficult to fantasise about the nakedness of a person when you have already seen them naked. Sexologists say that those couples who are not particularly in a hurry and spend some time on the platonic and erotic stages, turn out to be much more durable in the future. That fantasy foundation that they build together helps the couple to live through those numerous crises, of which there will be many in family life. For various reasons, direct sexual contact between partners can be difficult, but the psyche retains the emotional attraction and affection. Then, after the crisis has passed, sexual relations can be resumed, and the couple survives; they did not break up, since they were connected by much more than just the physiological side of their sexual relationship. Those couples who were in a hurry most often cannot survive the crisis together and break up.

Today, in a society that has become much more sexually liberated, sexual problems have not diminished at all. In the third book, we will talk more about family crises and those difficult moments when sexual attraction within a couple begins to fade. This is natural, when the partners have been together for a long time, and they have studied every centimetre of each other's bodies. And naturally, someone in the outside world may begin to cause more sexual attraction than their own partner. The question is how the couple deals with it. There are several different strategies. Sometimes partners agree to introduce an additional game element into their sex life in order to increase arousal. Sometimes spouses go to a professional sexologist to work through this crisis together. But most often, the usual splitting of their attraction occurs, which is experienced quite painfully; one of the partners gets a lover unilaterally. Then all emotional attraction and affection goes to the spouse, and all sexuality and drive is delegated to the lover.

If we are talking about a man, then he might idolise his wife. She acquires from him a certain icon-like image of a holy woman, a divine mother, but at the same time an absolutely asexual person. Simultaneously, the lover becomes a kind of devil, with whom he can explore all the dark corners of his fantasies and desires. There is no consensus on which is better. However, if a couple is at a high level of awareness and trust in each other, sometimes they can make a rational agreement to have another sexual life in addition to their life together, but according to very strict rules and boundaries. In my practice, I have worked with couples who have allowed each other lovers, provided that this is done as secretly and carefully as possible in relation to the spouse. That is, these adventures should in no way endanger the life of the family. Again, I'm not saying this is good or bad. Moreover, this is an extremely rare case. Most often, one of the partners simply starts a secret sex life and stops sex with the spouse. The second partner remains completely bewildered, and, of course, feels everything. After such a long period together, it is rarely possible to cheat secretly. These things are most often felt and experienced very painfully. That is why it is called a family crisis.

Such crises are brought very frequently to tarot consultations. The client sees an expert in the tarot reader, and in all areas, so the client definitely comes for so-called "normalisation". The client encounters some oddity in their behaviour or in the lives of their loved ones and, as a rule, becomes very anxious because they do not understand how dangerous what they are facing is. Since it is difficult to talk about sex and the client has no one to share their problems with, and there is not much high-quality information available, why not ask these questions to a tarologist? In the field of sexology, the client may be concerned about any number of issues. "How long should sexual intercourse last? After all, friends, and heroes in the movies, have sex all day long, but I can't do that. There must be something wrong with me." "Am I gay if I have sexual fantasies about my sister's husband? I'm married too! What should I do now, divorce?" Mothers are usually alarmed by their children's sexual play. They can wind themselves up so much that they see pathology and punish children for something absolutely ordinary. For example, children may show their genitals to each other. A separate topic is masturbation, around which a huge number of false myths have accumulated.

These are not therapy issues but simply counselling or even general sex education issues. And if the tarologist is confident in the information that they give the client, then, probably, there is nothing wrong with answering these questions. But once again I repeat: tarologists must be very clearly aware of the limits of their competence. It is always better to refer a client with a serious sexual problem to a professional who can really understand the problem and offer the right solution.

But if a professional sexologist masters the tool of tarot, then their work with cards on the topic of sexology can become truly unique. They will be able to quickly correlate the meanings of the arcana with all their professional knowledge, leading to interpretations of the cards that are really deep and accurate. They will be able to support their answers with correct knowledge and rely on cases from their professional practice. And they will not need an erotic deck to work with a sexual question; I am sure that they would just choose a neutral deck for such work.

# SECTION 6. USEFUL TERMS

## Libido – Eros – Thanatos

When we try to understand a particular term, difficulties can sometimes arise. This is especially the case when the term is introduced into usage for the first time, and when the one who introduces it is also a kind of pioneer in his field. This definitely applies to Sigmund Freud, who revolutionised psychotherapy. The terms that he introduced into the psychotherapeutic vocabulary have remained in it to this day. An important thing to remember is that throughout his life, Freud himself revised and corrected the meanings of those terms several times.

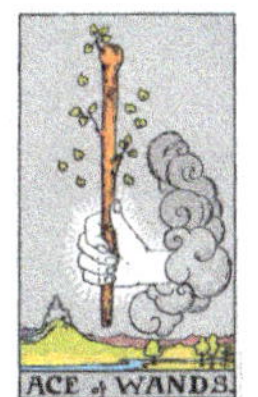


Initially, "libido" was understood as some kind of mental energy that underlies sexual desire. This concept can be understood narrowly and broadly. On the one hand, when talking about our adult understanding of sexuality, the energy of the libido can only be discharged as a result of sexual satisfaction. But there is a broader interpretation, in which libido is understood as any manifestations of attraction and love, including that of children to their parents and vice versa.

It was not so easy for Freud to convey his revolutionary views and ideas to the minds of the bourgeois society of Vienna. When he talked about sexuality and children at the same time, he was often misunderstood. But if we begin to understand sexuality to refer to the principle of pleasure, then Freud's theory of libido immediately becomes clearer. Everyone strives for pleasure, including babies. Therefore, the sexuality of an infant is interpreted as a way of obtaining pleasure in infancy.

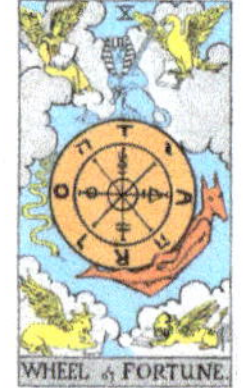


Freud spoke of various stages of psychosexual development in which the libido energy is associated with a certain area of the body. Through this, it becomes clear why so much is oral, anal and phallic in psychoanalytic literature. Of course, the main pleasure experienced by the baby is breastfeeding. We can say that the baby is at the oral stage, since it is the mouth that is the area in which the libido is concentrated. Then in the anal stage, the energy moves to the area of the sphincters, which are responsible for defecation and urination. The child enjoys the fact that at this moment they are learning to control these processes. Next is the phallic stage, in which the Oedipus complex will unfold. We'll talk about it a little later. Then the latent and genital stages. At any of these stages, fixation can occur if the libido energy for whatever reason cannot be properly discharged. Furthermore, according to Freud, this fixation leads to the formation of a certain character within the adult. For example, the oral character is directly related to the oral stage—if, of course, we consider everything in the paradigm of psychoanalysis. An obsessive-compulsive nature is related to the anal stage. And the histrionic character, which we have considered in this part, is definitely phallic in nature.

The energy of the libido, among other things, can be sublimated; that is, discharged not necessarily through sexual satisfaction but through substitutive forms, for example, creativity. If the energy of the libido is blocked and does not find a natural outlet, according to Freud, this leads to various kinds of neuroses and disorders.

Jung considered the libido a little more broadly. He did not associate this concept only with sexuality but saw it through the prism of Oriental philosophies. For him, libido was a form of psychic energy, such as qi in China or prana in India.

In my opinion, the concept of Eros is very close to libido. If we can generally understand Eros as the drive to life, then Thanatos is the opposite: a drive to death. Or you can formulate it a little differently: Eros is an attraction to creation, and Thanatos is an attraction to destruction. From this perspective, we can reduce all human impulses to these two poles. They are opposite in nature, and, in the spirit of psychoanalytic theory, create a certain balance of tension within a person. If Eros leads us to relationships, creativity and self-preservation, then Thanatos is expressed as aggression and destruction. The energy of Thanatos can be directed to the outside world as everything dark and destructive that a person is capable of. But it can also be directed to the inner world. Then we get a tendency towards self-aggression, sadism and masochism. Every time we ourselves sabotage our own pleasure and well-being, we are experiencing a similar manifestation of Thanatos.

Very many paradigms of psychology say that the human psyche can be split into two opposite poles, but they always say that a person should strive to integrate them. The defence mechanism of splitting must be processed into ambivalence so that a person can rely on a more holistic understanding of himself and the world around him. Death, as a phenomenon, is always associated with fear. From childhood, a person sacrifices his Thanatos to society, as they are obliged to restrain their destructive and aggressive impulses. But the price of such splitting off is often the rejection of death as a natural aspect of life. Within the framework of a rather interesting direction of body-oriented psychotherapy called "Thanatotherapy", they work to overcome such disintegration. Techniques include the person's progressive bodily relaxation, as well as their modelling of various symbolic deaths, in order to release and integrate repressed feelings. The symbolic experience of dying is not necessarily associated with physical death. In fact, it is about any kind of letting go, completion and separation, and it applies to a huge range of different situations. It is falling asleep, an orgasm, and madness. The fact is that some people have such a powerful emotional block when it comes to the theme of death that they can get stuck in situations that have long outlived their usefulness. They cannot let old elements of their lives die to make room for the new and useful.

Meditation as a technique for working with the inner world has long been successfully used by psychologists, although it originates in Hinduism. Even in the yoga tradition, there are special techniques aimed at the symbolic experience of death. This is necessary to weaken the attachment to one's own material nature and get closer to one's own spiritual principle. If a person can, in meditation, live through their own dying, at all stages and in all details, they receive a very powerful emotional experience, which reduces their attachment to their own ego. Of course, the mystical and psychotherapeutic traditions have different starting points here, as they are based on different pictures of the world. But both systems believe that death is a natural side of life that should not be emotionally alienated. In this matter, psychology and esotericism are in solidarity.

## Oedipus Complex

This is a very interesting and, in my opinion, important concept. An Oedipus complex occurs at the age of 3–5 years, when a child lives through the most important stage of their psychosexual development. Let's see what happens to the child during this period. At this point, the child already understands very well that they have a father and mother. This understanding was not there before; as we remember, up to a certain stage the whole world is concentrated exclusively in the mother figure. Now there are two parental figures, and there is a relationship between them that the child is trying to comprehend. The child already has some idea of whether he is a boy or a girl. At this point, the child faces two very difficult tasks. On the one hand, the child needs to identify with their same-gender parent. The boy must understand that he is like his father, and the parents must recognise this. Or, the girl must realise that she is the same as her mother, and again you need to get parental confirmation of this. And then the competition for the parent of the opposite sex begins, which in the case of a boy will be called the Oedipus complex, and in the case of a girl, the Electra complex.

While this is a psychosexual stage of development, we are talking about children who are only 3–5 years old. Their understanding of sexuality comes down to rather infantile and innocent fantasies. They just want to be admired and shown emotional attention. If Mum or Dad shows admiration on their faces when they see the child, then this is just what the child needs. At this age, the child simply copies what they see in a naive manner, and as they understand it. If Dad hugs Mum, and Mum looks at Dad in some special way, then the child needs to do the same. At this age, children are quite demonstrative. They really need attention. Also, they show jealousy. The girl can push away her mother, whom her father decided to kiss, and begins to kiss her father herself. It's not about sex at all. This is how a child imitates adult affection. From the outside, everything looks like an innocent game. But Freud was a genius when he described the psychosexual development of the child during this period because very often it is wrongly experienced in families, which can lead to the child having serious problems in building relationships in the future.

Let's talk a little more about Freud's terms. He wrote about the fear of castration. What did he mean?

When a boy competes with his father for his mother, he is afraid that he will be punished for this. Castration here is symbolic. The father, simply in retaliation for this competition, does not recognise the boy as a man. A mother may punish her daughter in the same way if she does not understand why the girl behaves so "provocatively" during this period. The Oedipus complex is an internal conflict in a child. How to get recognition from the parent of the opposite sex and at the same time not be punished by the parent of the same sex. Here, of course, everything depends on the parents, who sometimes make just monstrous mistakes during this sensitive period.

The child will behave extremely persistently in an attempt to be liked. A girl might simply not leave her father, dance, or imitate some seductive movements that she saw somewhere. Some mothers get furious and punish their daughters very harshly for such behaviour. They may regard them as real rivals, a real threat, not realising that before them is just an innocent child. It can happen that the mother cannot come to terms with the fact that she is ageing, and the girl is full of life and energy. And it also happens that the father symbolically seduces the girl by overexciting her with inappropriate touches, supposedly in the game, so the child is faced with an affect that she simply cannot process.

The Oedipus/Electra complex must be lived through with the help of the parents. Usually, psychologists during this period suggest doing the following. The father should say to the girl: "You are my beautiful and beloved daughter. I love you very much and cherish you. But my woman is your mother. And when you grow up, you will definitely find yourself a man who will also love and cherish you." And, importantly, the mother must agree with this. Exactly the same text can be pronounced to a boy by the mother. This will allow the complex to resolve properly. First, the child gets what they wanted—admiration and love. Secondly, a line is clearly drawn within the family system. Thirdly, the parent of the same gender recognises the child and does not punish them. If parents help their child during this period, the child will not be so prone to triangulation in the future. A woman will not be so attracted to married men, and a man to married women. This scenario of competition and recognition was completed in their childhood.

## Sexualisation

Sexualisation is quite an interesting mechanism. The fact is that we very often experience excitement for one reason or another, but arousal can be about anything. We can experience a normal physiological arousal when we are hungry, thirsty or want to stretch muscles that are numb. We may experience psychological arousal: be anxious, annoyed or interested in something. The problem begins at the moment when we cannot correctly interpret the cause of our arousal. For example, when we feel scared or anxious, we need support, but some people register this internal arousal and confuse it with physical hunger. They go to the refrigerator and start eating instead of turning to another person for help.

This confusion occurs because when faced with problems we often regress to earlier stages of development. Why not regress to the oral stage, where the child received pleasure and security through feeding? Then, when the adult eats, they really feel better. But if they are not aware of what exactly is happening here, they risk reinforcing this pattern in their behaviour, which will lead to problems later.

Sexualisation works in a similar way. Excitation, which was originally not sexual at all, is registered by a person as sexual arousal. And then exactly the same thing happens that we described in the example with food. Quite often in couples, it happens that partners avoid experiencing any difficult feelings for each other by having sex. Sex is one of the aggressive forms of behaviour, and it is how you can really win back your own aggression. But the problem is that the couple do not realise what they are feeling. As in the case of food, a person emasculates their inner world, their sensitivity and awareness become dull, and their behaviour becomes compulsive. Unfortunately, this mechanism is very often exploited in sales today. Even when advertising something non-sexual, a sexy model is always chosen. It is an attempt to sexualise, energise and create lust for a product that has no sexual function. But our psyche really recognises it as more noticeable and attractive. There is definitely no harm in this if we realise that this is what's happening.

## Perversions

This term is not so easy to define, since it is connected with the concept of the norm, which is rather problematic in psychology. In the third book, we will talk about this in great detail. For now, we will only hint at the fact that there is no single understanding of the norm in psychology. It is always historically and culturally conditioned. This is especially evident in the question of sexual perversions. What is a "perversion"? It is "love in reverse", if we consider the original Latin meaning of the term. That is, a person with a perversion receives sexual satisfaction in some unconventional and distorted way. Historically, when sex was considered exclusively from a pragmatic point of view, namely as a way to procreate, any sexual practices that did not lead to this—namely masturbation, homosexuality or oral sex—were considered perversions. Time has passed, and today no one looks at the issue from this point of view. But the essence of the term remains the same.

The pervert does experience some shift in sexual drive. A good example would be fetishism, when a man is attracted not so much by a female body as by some attribute or accessory, for example, high heels, leather clothes or bright red lipstick. All elements of bondage or sadomasochism also fall into this category.

It should be noted that we are not talking about this issue from the point of view of morality. Sex in today's world has quite obvious ethical boundaries. The use of elements of violence with the informed consent of all participants in the sexual act is not illegal. It is a different matter when there is forced sex or sexual exploitation of people who cannot give informed consent, such as people with mental disabilities or children. Here, everyone will agree that this is a crime.

Such topics very rarely become the subject of tarot consultations. Sexuality is a very intimate and closed topic, and the client rarely brings it up for discussion. It is simply important to emphasise here that each person's sexual desire developed in absolutely unique conditions. What attracts one person may even repel another. But there is no need to rush to evaluate perversions, since this is still the prerogative of psychiatrists.

A tarot reader may have his own moral view of what is normal and what is a perversion in sexual behaviour. And here, in my opinion, the tarologist should adhere to the following rule: you cannot force yourself to analyse sexual topics that seem unpleasant to you, even if society does not consider them to be immoral. You will simply be useless as a tarot reader in such an analysis, as you will remain closed internally.

## Erotic Transference

I won't say anything new here. The concept of transference and countertransference was discussed in great detail in the first part of this book. The fact is that it can be experienced as a feeling of love. This often happens, for example, in a teacher-student or consultant-client relationship, which is why we are talking about it again.

A person can experience erotic transference in varying degrees of intensity. On the one hand, it can have only a slight tinge of love and eroticism, which distinguishes it from all other types of transference. On the other hand, it can take on very intense and negative forms, and then it really creates serious problems.

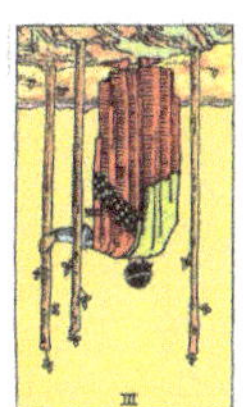

Since this transference usually takes place in a context in which sexual relations are impossible and unethical, a person's fantasies cannot be tested by reality. In theory, we remember that the transference continues to persist until the person sees a difference between the figure from their past who is the source of the transference, and the person opposite, to whom the transference is addressed. Over time, this "magic" dissipates as the differences become too obvious. But if the transference is based on sexual attraction, even if it is very childish in nature, it may last longer and be more concentrated, since it contains a large focus of internal excitation.

In the work of a tarot reader, erotic transference can also arise. If the practitioner unconsciously turns on the reverse countertransference, then the accuracy of the reading will be greatly reduced. Any feelings in the countertransference cloud the vision. Here, it is not just feelings, but a reciprocal strong attraction that does not allow you to work adequately.

## Reaction Formation

In the next book, we will discuss in detail the mechanisms of psychological defence. But there are so many of these mechanisms that some can be discussed right now, especially since reactive formation is often turned on precisely in an attempt to protect the consciousness and ego from unwanted sexual impulses.

The essence of this mechanism is that a person begins to transform a negative feeling into a positive one, or vice versa. Realising a real feeling is dangerous, and this mechanism works to protect a person from this. For example, consider when a second child is born in a family. If the age difference between the children is not very big, about 3–5 years, then a real disaster occurs for the first child. The first child has not yet got rid of the idea of their own omnipotence; they are the centre of the universe. And then someone else is born, and the parents naturally turn all their attention to the newborn. The normal reaction of a child to such an event is rage. But the child cannot express it, as it will not be supported by his parents. And then the older child begins to love the younger one emphatically. The child takes an active part in caring for their sibling, takes them in their arms and begins to rock them so actively that the child seems to be shaking the spirit out of the baby. The child's love for a brother or sister is a reaction formation—the translation of a feeling of hatred into love.

And exactly the opposite can happen, when love is transformed into hatred and aggression. For example, a man may have sexual feelings for someone, but he cannot show them openly. These feelings may be contrary to his own moral code or not supported by society. For example, this attraction may be to another man or to a dissolute woman. Reaction formation will be expressed by such a man not only disliking gay men or prostitutes, but actively organising their persecution. Usually, such people are at the head of some communities that fight against "immorality". But in fact, these people are trying to cope with their own forbidden impulses that would be dangerous for the ego.

You may have come across the type of militant scientist who despises any manifestation of esotericism. He does not just despise, but launches a whole public campaign with the aim of subjecting all esotericists to almost the inquisition. Of course, in modern society, no one will allow the inquisition, but the scientist is always welcome to write an aggressive article, to declare all esotericists charlatans or crazy, or to discredit someone's name. At the same time, there are many scientists who do not care about esotericism at all. If it causes such a powerful rejection, and a person spends so much time and energy on his anti-esoteric activity, then it is worth suspecting that some kind of protective mechanism is hidden in his behaviour, most likely a reaction formation.

# SECTION 7. REFLECTION ON A PRACTICAL CASE

## EMPRESS TAKES OFF HER CROWN, CHAPTER 6

That evening, Emma and John went out into town to shop, pick out Christmas presents—as Christmas was only a couple of weeks away—and have dinner somewhere along the way. Everything around was decorated with multicoloured lights. The shop windows were lit up in a festive way, but Emma couldn't relax. When they entered a store, she found herself choosing gifts somehow abstractly, indifferently. John, on the other hand, looked like a happy child. He fooled around, trying on Christmas hats in every store, sometimes with deer antlers, sometimes with little bells. Emma smiled, took pictures of him, and then went back to her thoughts.

When they finished shopping, they were already quite cold, tired and hungry, so they began to look for a suitable place for dinner.

"Maybe here?" John pointed to a small restaurant. It was also decorated for Christmas. There were pink garlands and balloons everywhere, and in a window display stood a snow-white unicorn with shiny gold-dusted hooves.

Emma grimaced in disgust. "Anywhere but here," she protested. "I'm going to be sick of the colour pink for a couple of weeks."

"Whatever works for you," John said and unlocked his phone to look at the photos that he'd taken during the walk.

Emma looked around and chose a traditional pub that looked like Scrooge against the Christmas kaleidoscope. There were fewer people there, and Emma dragged John inside.

They sat down at a table, looked through the menu, chose and made an order.

"Are you tired?" John asked. "You're kind of sad today."

"Not exactly tired," Emma said. "The last client ruined my mood."

John nodded in understanding. "I know what you mean—I've got a couple of clients like that. But it's work. You've got to grin and bear it."

He and Emma hadn't discussed difficult clients very often before. And Emma clung to the topic, hoping she could clarify for herself what exactly was disturbing her.

"And how many clients do you have now?"

"Ten, not counting Tom," John answered, folding either a gnome or a deer out of a napkin. His playfulness never went away, and he looked carefree and easy, like a child taken to his favourite amusement park. "Why do you ask?"

"How many of them are unpleasant for you?" Emma said.

John thought for a moment, ceasing to torture the napkin.

"I would single out two," he said. "There is one guy who's constantly late for training. He ruins my schedule. He'll demand that I set aside a certain hour for him, and then he won't turn up, or only does at the end. He does pay if he misses it, of course. It just pisses me off. It feels a bit disrespectful, really."

"And the other one?" Emma asked.

"I have one client, a girl. She's already blown my brains out. She will watch some videos on the internet, and then start talking about how to do the exercises. I explain to her that you can't do this, otherwise you will ruin your joints. But she is stubborn. I feel like she's constantly competing with me. I get angry then—I mean, if you're so smart, why the hell do you need a coach at all? Go on your own and do it yourself, and then you can heal what you damage yourself as well."

Emma began to feel the conversation bringing her to her senses somewhat. Before, she could not emerge from her gloomy mood, but now energy had risen from somewhere and she wanted to follow it.

"Tell me, do you have any clients who look like Barbie prostitutes?"

John looked at Emma in surprise. He didn't quite understand what she was talking about.

"Well, you know," she said. "Really artificial, lisping, all in pink. Who are only about money and sex and prey on rich men."

John smiled and nodded.

"There are enough of them," he said. "I have one of them, although my colleagues have more. They don't stay for long with me."

"Why?"

John pointed to himself with a silent question on his face, saying, *Do you even see me?* But Emma was still restless. She still couldn't shake the mixed feeling of anxiety and irritation.

"What's wrong with you?" she asked.

"No, that's not the point here," John said. "Outwardly, perhaps they would be interested in me. But their erogenous zone is a wallet. And we in the gym are definitely not the most enviable suitors in this regard. In general, they look at us as service personnel."

"Do they flirt with you?" Emma asked.

"They flirt with everyone!" John blurted out. "They don't know how to talk any other way."

"And you?"

"And I flirt back," John said.

Emma pouted in resentment. She really didn't like her boyfriend's answer. She imagined Susie in her clattering heels, wagging her hips, pacing the gym and theatrically throwing up her pink-manicured hands. *"Ah, give me a dumbbell! Oh, is it right for me to hold my arse when I squat!"*

John noticed the change in her mood and immediately added, "My job is to flirt. Why are you surprised?"

"I don't get it," Emma said. "And if she starts pestering you sexually, is that also your job?"

John looked surprised.

"They definitely won't," he said. "That's the point. They will make eyes, smile, wag their booty, but nothing more than that. Well, I am required to smile, to compliment, to help them feel beautiful."

"But why? Are they beautiful?"

"It's the service industry," John protested. "They should feel welcome, that they are getting the attention they came for. You know, they don't really piss me off for one reason: if they come to the gym, then they work really hard. This is exactly what I've noticed. I had such a girl among my clients last year. Of course, she was constantly flirting, as constantly as she breathes. But when it came to training, she beat a lot of my male clients. Grabbed her dumbbells and silently got on with it. It was hard for her—she was puffing all over—but she pursed her lips and kept going. I respect that. It's much worse when they come here so smart and sure of themselves, and no matter what I ask, they'll do the opposite to prove that they are so independent and free. Why do they have to come to the gym to prove it? It's difficult with those women. You give her an exercise, and she will make you almost defend your dissertation in order to prove to her that this is exactly the exercise that suits her."

John spoke with feeling, somewhat annoyed. It was clear that he thought deeply about his work.

"And have you ever thought about… I don't know, having an affair with a client who tried to seduce you?"

John paused, glared at Emma, then broke into a smile.

"Are you jealous?" he drawled, smiling like a Cheshire Cat. "Yes, you're jealous, that's for sure."

Emma was very embarrassed. But John lay down on the table, put his head on his hands and looked up at her with the same look dogs give owners who've come to pet them. If the guy had had a tail, he would have actively wagged it.

"Well, all right, I'm jealous." Emma surrendered.

"Oh, tell me how jealous you are!" He did not let up. "Well, come on, come on, tell me what you imagine when you are jealous!"

Emma couldn't help but smile. A certain sense of unrestrained playfulness swept over her, too. If this conversation began strained and anxious, now it had turned into some kind of exciting game. Emma leaned back in her chair, looked languidly at John, and spoke.

"Well, you are standing in the gym."

"Standing handsomely?"

"Yes, you stand handsomely and sexily."

"Go on."

"And everyone is looking at you. What strong arms you have, and how tall and muscular you are. And they think how they can touch you. And then such a beauty appears, who passes by you, pauses and winks at you, and you… wink at her too."

John looked at Emma carefully.

"And that's it, you're under hypnosis." Emma felt that the game was becoming not so pleasant.

"You know, I'm jealous of you too," John admitted. "Male clients come to your house, for one-on-one sessions. Do you know what thoughts go through my head?"

"What thoughts?"

"Like the pictures in your erotic cards."

"You know I don't work with that deck with clients, it's just for the collection." Emma took John by the hand.

He took her hands in his, leaned over the table, looked intently into her eyes, and with complete seriousness, said clearly, "So I don't play with dolls either."

A wave of heat ran down Emma's spine. Such an obvious comparison put everything in its place. She remembered Susie and now saw in her not at all a sexy adult woman, but a child who'd climbed into her mother's wardrobe and makeup bag. She even felt sorry for her.

"Listen," she said to John. "I think I offended a client today."

"Well, it happens," he said. "Sometimes they just ask for it. But after that, it still feels bad. Will there be consequences?"

"I don't think so. She just won't come back, that's all the consequences."

"Maybe it's for the best."

The waiter brought their order and they began to eat. Emma hadn't realised she was so hungry. Now she ate her lasagne greedily, feeling how her whole body seemed to respond to everything that was happening around her: to the colours, the sounds of medieval music, the smell of food. She looked at John, and could not get out of her head those fantasies that she'd begun to voice. But now, she is the one who comes to his gym, and he chooses only her from all the others. They walk together, and he does not take his eyes off her. He hugs her, and everyone around just turns green with envy.

# SECTION 8. PRACTICAL RECOMMENDATIONS

## PRACTICAL ANALYSIS OF CHAPTERS 5 AND 6

Of course, Emma is right; this was not her best work. This often happens when a client brings a difficult problem for a tarot reader, and the tarot reader simply cannot work to the best of their ability. Their own psychological material begins to come to the surface and makes it difficult to concentrate on work. Emma read the cards absolutely correctly, but she did not have enough experience and strength to manage the psychological side of the consultation.

1. The histrionic client is a test for the tarot reader. But here a lot depends on what gender the tarologist is. Such clients (in 99 percent of cases they are women) behave completely differently with men and women. If the tarologist is a man, then the client will do everything possible and impossible to please him. In this case, everything will be like a theatrical scene of seduction. It is difficult for men to concentrate on work in such a scenario, as they are almost transparently offered something completely different. The client will flirt, stare languidly, ask provocative questions and expect a sexual response from the practitioner. But the trap, as we remember, lies precisely in the fact that the client approaches the consultation sexually, but this is not at all what she needs. If the tarologist cannot resist and begins to respond to such invitations, believing that he is dealing with a conscious and adult woman, he will injure her. The most correct behaviour is to recognise such a woman, notice her desire to impress and please, perhaps give a little positive feedback and compliments, but in no case cross the sexual line. If a male tarologist manages to cope with his own excitement and sees a child in front of him in the body of an adult woman, then he can provide the client with tremendous

psychological help. All she wants is to be liked by a man, and not pay for it with sex.

2. If the tarot reader is a woman, then, most likely, the client will behave more like a child or a little sister. The test is also difficult, but it is of a completely different nature. A histrionic client often evokes strong irritation in adult women and a desire to punish and symbolically castrate her. Of course, this is the effect of countertransference. A tarot reader may unconsciously feel like a mother whose daughter is behaving indecently. Sometimes envy may even turn on, as such clients covertly give the female tarot reader the message: "I am more beautiful than you." If the tarologist manages to cope with her own irritation and again see a child in front of her in the body of an adult woman, then the attitude changes. The client wants to be liked by the female tarologist in her femininity and sexuality, not with the aim of seducing her but of receiving female initiation or recognition as an equal instead of someone who needs to be punished.

3. Emma couldn't quite control her irritation. At least she said, "Don't you hear yourself?" rather than "You should have seen yourself." Such wording would be much more hurtful for a client who is especially invested in her appearance. But Emma could not support the client. She showed reluctance to help her. And the client, who was a vulnerable and sensitive child inside, felt it very quickly.

4. It's no surprise that such a client comes with a list of men. It is also not surprising that none of them suit her. Emma was absolutely right when she drew attention to an abundance of reversed court cards and symbols associated with children. Of course, it is not necessary to encourage such a client to keep on pursuing men like these—otherwise there's simply no point to the tarot consultation. The question is how to properly encourage such a client to see the problems with their approach to relationships. It is usually recommended to invite the client to ask the cards the question: "What makes me a valuable partner in a relationship?" By the way, it is absolutely not a fact that this spread will be negative. But as experienced tarot readers, we know that any card can be interpreted in a positive or negative way, as well as at different levels of maturity. If the client agrees to such a question, then the tarologist can interpret the answer precisely in the vein of adult

femininity and sexuality. For the client, this will be a completely new experience of acceptance and reflection. She begins to hear about qualities that she did not consider valuable.

5. In the previous part, when we discussed the narcissistic client, we talked about how dangerous it is for the tarologist to share their own personal information and experiences with the client. This can lead to a great danger of being devalued. Of course, we remember that there are no pure characters, and a histrionic client can also be a narcissist. But it's usually noticeable in how much they idealise you. A real histrionic will never cover you in compliments. They are on stage, not you. Therefore, if histrionic features prevail in the client, you do not need to be afraid of subsequent devaluation. Either way, it won't be as painful as it is with narcissists.

If you are sure that you are dealing with a histrionic client, then it is very important that you share personal experiences with them. It may not be worth talking about your relationships, but you can always give a real example from life of a relationship built on healthy attachment and adult sexuality. A histrionic character may have a real shortage of healthy role models. And a tarot reader can provide such an example, emphasising its value.

6. Susie is certainly a difficult case. The problem is that she did not bring other topics to the consultation, only the choice of men. If a histrionic client asks about something else that's not related to her relationships with men, then it is possible and necessary to emphasise the client's independence and maturity in this area as much as possible. It can be anything. A client, for example, may absolutely not be able to choose men correctly, but she may have the right view on some financial issue, competence in a particular profession (even if she herself does not consider it valuable), experience in travelling, in fitness, in dealing with animals. Anything where the histrionic scheme does not work, and where the client managed to become an adult. There will definitely be such areas in the client's life; she just might not openly demonstrate them. The tarologist can emphasise such areas so that the client can notice these strengths and learn to rely on them.

7. The histrionic character is by no means the most difficult client if the tarologist clearly understands that they are watching a play. Histrionic characters are good actors and can mislead a

specialist. They love the role they play much more than they love themselves. If you help these clients to remember that they do not live on stage, that there are a lot of valuable things about them in addition to the role they play, then they will greatly benefit from tarot consultation.

# SECTION 9. TRAPS AND DANGERS

## Psychosomatics: A Scientific and Esoteric View

Scientists are extremely cautious people. They are accustomed to double-checking everything multiple times before asserting something with complete certainty. Mistakes are possible, but the very procedure for checking knowledge in the scientific environment is very meticulous, and the rule of peer review and opponent criticism forces scientists to consider literally every word they write.

Of course, there are no such rules in esoteric culture. Therefore, the different ways of viewing certain esoteric phenomena may differ not so much in essence as in scope. We have already mentioned that scientists do not recognise many diseases as actually psychosomatic. Alexander's Classic Seven suggests that confirmation and evidence have been found regarding these ailments. However, the fact that other diseases are not considered psychosomatic does not mean that there is no such connection. Rather, it should be understood as follows: there is no scientific evidence of the psychosomatic basis of other diseases yet.

This is where the esotericist will start arguing heatedly. They may wonder why a similar mechanism works for, say, ulcerative colitis, but does not work for, say, urolithiasis. Is the body really so selective in the symptoms through which it speaks to its master? This is a difficult question, but among esotericists there is often an opinion that absolutely all diseases are psychosomatic in nature, and due to the fact that the scientific picture of the world is significantly different, the esotericist interprets this phenomenon in a slightly different way.

In esotericism, the physical body is given a subordinate role. The more subtle the nature of a person is, the more power it has over more material bodies. There is a completely understandable logic in this, which even scientists are able to admit in part. Spiritual values significantly influence a person's thoughts. Their mental attitude dictates the feeling that any particular situation evokes. And the feeling, in turn, dictates the corresponding bodily reaction.

It turns out that the deeper we go into matter, the more subordinate a relationship we see. As a result, it turns out that the physical body and its state (health) are the sum of the influences of all the more subtle bodies: spirit, soul, thoughts and feelings (there can be more of these subtle bodies, since everything depends on a certain esoteric classification).

Esotericism will assert the following: illness never begins in the physical body. The cause must always be sought in the subtle bodies. If the imbalance is not found and corrected there, it will gradually manifest itself on more and more material planes until it becomes noticeable. This means it is possible to work with the disease from both ends. On the one hand, it is possible to treat the body directly, which traditional Western medicine successfully does. But, on the other hand, one cannot ignore the subtle cause of the disease. Traditional doctors do not pay any attention to this at all, and then the diseases become chronic, recurring, hereditary. All this, from an esoteric perspective, indicates that the true root of the problem has gone unnoticed and has not been eliminated.

One can argue against this because doctors still show wonderful results and many diseases do not return at all, although they were treated only physically. But there is also a counterargument here. During the period of illness, the inner world of a person changes very much. There is often a strong existential shake-up of the personality. The very fact that an ill person cannot lead their former way of life, but is forced to lie down and think about their condition, mentally knocks them out of the model in which they previously lived. It cannot be said that diseases do not change the inner world of a person, but sometimes they are not enough to get to and work out the "subtle cause" of a physical imbalance. And as soon as the person feels better, the desire to delve into oneself and look for answers to uncomfortable questions disappears sharply.

Perhaps in the future, science will expand the list of psychosomatic diseases. And then medicine will change somewhat and become a little closer to the esoteric understanding of human nature. The very phenomenon of "psychosomatics" is already a huge step towards the scientific and esoteric world views working with each other.

What about tarot consultants? It is no secret that many practitioners consider the topic of health unpleasant, and some refuse to work with it at all. This is partly dictated by the fact that clients sometimes turn to avoidance behaviour and do not go to traditional doctors, choosing tarot consultations instead, until the disease is in too advanced a state to do something. However, if the client and tarologist insist on a holistic approach, then tarot consultation on the topic of health can be an excellent impetus for development. But here the angle changes a bit. It needs to be conveyed to the client that tarot cards are not MRIs or ultrasounds. They do not make a diagnosis, and if they do, it would be ethical to verify it using traditional medical diagnostics. But the question of how an already diagnosed disease is seen on subtle planes is the exclusive prerogative of the tarot and other mantic systems.

By combining tarot and traditional medicine, the client gets a complete picture and can work with the problem on many levels at once. They haven't cancelled their visit to the doctor or stopped taking their prescriptions, but they are also looking for connections between material and subtle ailments to solve the problem on both sides. It is important that the client takes this approach, otherwise they will shift all responsibility onto the tarot practitioner if something goes wrong.

Therefore, it is better not to diagnose diseases, but to look at what imbalance in the inner world lies behind this disease and look for ways to understand and eliminate it.

# SECTION 10. PSYCHOLOGICAL PARADIGM

## Existential Paradigm

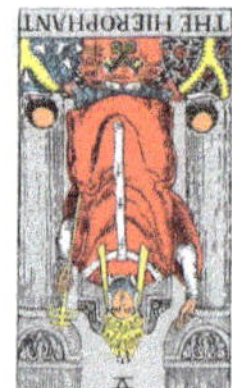

It may seem that the philosophy of existentialism is most contrary to esotericism. One can easily imagine how an existential psychotherapist and, for example, a tarot practitioner might clash in a serious dispute. But these two views do not so radically contradict each other. Yes, indeed, they suggest two completely different pictures of the world. But often this is exactly what we encounter in our tarot consultations. A client arriving for an appointment with an esotericist does not necessarily have an esoteric world view. Quite often it turns out that the client comes exactly so as to avoid collision with some existential truths. Namely, it may not be clear to them how to live in the world if there is no mysticism in it.

Perhaps we can best understand the essence of the existential paradigm if we understand that the key word in this paradigm is the word "being". The human psyche is not seen as a solid structure, but a continuous, changing process of "becoming". There are three worlds in which our existence takes place, and each is designated by a German word. Umwelt is the involvement of man, as a biological being, in natural diversity. Mitwelt is the embeddedness of a person in a wide social context. And finally, Eigenwelt is a person's experience of their self or their inner world.

Existential psychology deals with the complex problems of being. It considers a person as a creature limited by the scientific picture of the world. Imagine that there are no Higher Forces, no reincarnation, karma, tarot or astrology that can help a person with an esoteric world view so much. There is only man and the world around him, in which he is doomed to be.

What will such a person face? On the one hand, they are doomed to experience social relationships, and on the other hand, to loneliness, since they cannot claim full acceptance in society and at the same time maintain their uniqueness. This is one of the most important topics in working in the existential paradigm—how to maintain this complex balance. Lying is the surest way to lose authenticity and replace being-for-oneself with being-for-others. We often lie to ourselves about who we are. And not less often, we lie about ourselves to those around us, since the very idea of loneliness is totally unbearable for many. But the price for such a lie is very high. You lose your authenticity. No matter how hard you try to be accepted by society, full acceptance never happens. This is one of the complex existential truths—a person is doomed to loneliness in society.

The second problem is the finiteness of existence. This is where the main conflict with esotericism arises. We are not accustomed to believe that there is nothing beyond death. Any esoteric teaching is based on the axiom of posthumous existence, whether it is life on the subtle planes or reincarnation and rebirth. From an existential point of view, there is nothing beyond death, only emptiness. It is important to emphasise that the choice of world view is the right of every person. If a client does not believe in reincarnation, they cannot be persuaded otherwise. They may ask how you look at this issue, but your answer will not change their outlook overnight. In fact, clients need to be supported precisely within their own paradigm (perspective).

The tarot consultant in such a situation faces a problem. The tarologist knows how to deal with the fear of death in an esoteric picture of the world, but how do they do this if a person denies subtle planes? There are ways in existential therapy to deal with such questions, and they are no less effective than relying on an esoteric picture of the world. In particular, when experiencing loss, a person learns, on the one hand, to really say goodbye and let go of the departed, on the other hand, he learns to see the traces that we leave in the world. The person is remembered. Their features are visible in those close to them, especially in children. Some product of their activity or creativity remains after them. This is not an attempt to avoid the awareness of death and complete dissolution of the person as a phenomenon; this is the simultaneous farewell and awareness of new forms of being, but without the possibility of turning back time.

Next, the question of choice. Being human means constantly being faced with choices. Existentialists emphasise the complexity of such situations. The choice of one alternative will inevitably annul the other. And the problem is that a person will never know what would have happened if they had chosen the other one. Remember: the existentialist cannot lay out the cards and see which is better. There are no cards or other mantic systems. There is only adult responsibility for your choice and resignation to the fact that you will never be able to find out whether or not the choice was "correct".

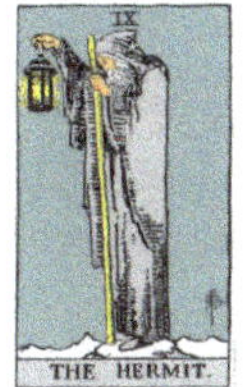


And, of course, the most difficult problem is one of meaning. In astrology, we can see what "task for incarnation" each individual client has. Tarot can also help us with this. There are no such clues in the existential picture of the world. But on the other hand, this is good. After all, there is a danger that the consultant will read the symbols incorrectly, and then the client will attempt to live their life in a way according to the wrong meaning and lose precious time. In this paradigm, understanding meaning comes with finding your authenticity. When a person has an adult understanding of who they are, the meaning of their life is found. This is not something static, chosen once and for all. This is living in the present moment and the ability to search for the meaning of our lives based on who we are today.

"What total pessimism!" the reader will exclaim. And they will only partially be right. Yes, indeed, the philosophy of existentialism looks in many ways gloomy and pessimistic. But in fact, existential psychologists enjoy life no less than other people. They just know how to face ordinary human limitations and difficulties and do not run away from them. Knowing who you are is a great blessing, and happy is the one who has managed to find and accept their authenticity.

And then it's a matter of world view. The existential paradigm leads a person to maturity (which, by the way, is very lacking for some esotericists). Whether there are subtle worlds or not is a matter of faith. At present, we cannot unequivocally prove either their presence or their absence. But working in counselling, we are obliged to admit that the client sitting opposite us may have a completely different picture of the world from ours. Is it necessary to "convert" the client to esotericism? That is a point of argument. The fact that the client came to us, on the one hand, allegedly gives us such a right. But on the other hand, they came for an opinion, perhaps for support, but certainly not for a "new ideological citizenship". A good consultant is always sensitive to such nuances. It is important to understand how what we say to the client will be refracted through their world view. Who takes responsibility for what happens during the consultation? Who makes the decision based on the cards? Who makes the choice? These are important questions that help find a common ground for a dialogue between esotericists and existential psychologists.

# SECTION 11. ESOTERIC ESSAY

## Sex and Esotericism

Sex is a very difficult topic to discuss in the context of esotericism. It seems that there is an impassable gulf between the esoteric tradition and the tendencies of the modern Western world, where many things are sexualised. The view on sex within different esoteric traditions needs to be understood correctly, since blindly following the advice of the classics can cause serious psychological harm to a beginner esoteric practitioner.

The fact is that a huge number of classical works on esotericism were written at a time when there was a serious taboo on the very topic of sexuality. Whether it was the Middle Ages or the Renaissance, when people were still afraid of the Inquisition, or the heyday of esotericism in the late 19th and early 20th centuries when theosophists worked, the topic of sexuality was often ignored. It should be mentioned that in the last century, Freud's theory of psychoanalysis had serious problems being accepted by the bourgeois society of that time, precisely because it placed a huge emphasis on sexuality.

If we read the biographies of many famous esotericists, a certain asexual image is formed. As if in the life of these great people there was no intimacy at all, neither in thoughts nor in practice, as in the case of Helena Blavatsky. And since these are significant figures that set a very high standard in esotericism, the illusion may arise that they should be imitated in literally everything, including their personality type and psychosexual behaviour. The mistake is that we live in a different age. The mystics of the past did not live in the sexually electrified field that we find ourselves in today. In addition, the psychological state of many of them generally leaves much to be desired. In character, Blavatsky was an extremely specific person, like Paracelsus, like John Dee. If these people found themselves in modern society, they would be considered, to put it mildly, strange or even "mentally ill". And not at all because of their engagement with the occult, but precisely because of their reactions to all other mundane topics.

The fact is that the sexual drive is one of the most powerful. It is important to understand it not only as an immediate need for sex but more broadly, as it is understood in psychoanalysis, when one speaks of Eros as opposed to Thanatos, or of the life instinct as opposed to the death instinct. Blind suppression of libido can entail a huge number of psychological problems, and many experts are convinced that, in principle, it is impossible to suppress and can only be successfully sublimated (replaced with a similar, but more socially approved, impulse).

In the history of esotericism, there is a vivid example of careless treatment of one's own sexuality. This is the case of the famous mystic, theosophist and clairvoyant Charles Leadbeater. Even during his lifetime, he was accused of molesting young boys, which he partially admitted himself. He said that, being a pupil in a religious school, he had been subjected to similar corruption and considered it the norm. And no matter how hard he tried to ignore his sexuality, which, in his case, was criminal, it still found a way out.

In modern esoteric literature, there are few works devoted to the topic of sexuality and spiritual growth. But there are still excellent examples, such as Jack Kornfield's *A Path with Heart*, where the author says that spiritual growth, cut off from ordinary life, is not the norm and that such a path entails a lot of problems. He refers to the fact that he personally knows many gurus who are experts in matters of mysticism, but their worldly personalities and lives make them extremely unpleasant and suffering people. Kornfield has an entire chapter devoted to the topic of sex and spiritual growth, where he writes that birds do it, bees do it, and most gurus do it, debunking the myth that the more spiritual a person is, the more asexual they become.

The point here is simply a reassessment of values. Indeed, if in the process of their development a person pays no less attention and respect to their sexuality than to everything else, then it will develop naturally and will not divert attention to itself as much as in the case of its severe repression. It's just that sex doesn't come first, and the sex drive doesn't guide the ego and can easily fade into the background when needed. One drive does not negate the others but is neatly synthesised into a single whole. Such a mystic will never say that sex is something special (uniquely good or uniquely bad); for them it is just another important side of human nature, the same as the need for food, sleep or acceptance.

Therefore, sexual behaviour requires the same attention as any other side of a person who has embarked on the path of spiritual development. These aspects of the self are not mutually exclusive, but complementary. Rigid treatment of one's sexuality most often leads to disorders and perversions, which certainly do not contribute to spiritual development. In the Indian tradition, we can read that a man leaves for the search for the spiritual until after he has realised himself in the mundane, in particular in family and sexual life. Even Buddha first married, fathered a son, lived in a palace and enjoyed all the pleasures of worldly life before he left in search of salvation from suffering. As you can see, examples in the spiritual tradition are different.

A path with heart, a metaphor chosen by Jack Kornfield as the title of his book, is an excellent reminder that spiritual development should not be at the expense of all other development, and the sexual nature of man is no exception.

# SECTION 12. PROBLEMS OF THE TAROT COMMUNITY

## From Inquisition to Discrimination

This section is not easy for me to write, perhaps due to the fact that the topic is very emotionally coloured. It is generally difficult to talk about discrimination, and certainly, no one wants to experience it at all. But I am sure that this topic needs to be discussed, even though it causes a lot of unpleasant feelings.

Let's start with some examples. Suppose you work in the esoteric sphere, and this is your main occupation and source of income. You have studied for a long time and continue to improve in your profession. You are legally registered and pay taxes. You deeply believe in what you do; esotericism is not just a profession, but also the basis of your entire world view. So many times in your work, you have encountered the gratitude of clients, their admiration and desire to come to you again. But then the following happens: you take a taxi, and a very sociable driver asks you what you do. Suddenly, something happens inside. Something stops you from answering quickly and proudly, from saying, "I am a tarot reader", "I am an astrologer", or "I am a Reiki healer". And you timidly tell the taxi driver some profession from your past, saying "I am an accountant", "I am a teacher", or "I am a translator". You have not done this job for a hundred years, but for some reason now you are hiding behind these past professional identities of yours.

Another case. You know your client in multiple overlapping contexts. Let's say you are relatives, school friends or colleagues in a second profession. At your consultation, he is a grateful client who really needs your help and an esoteric interpretation of his situation. But in a different context, for example, at a school reunion, a family dinner or a work seminar, he devalues esotericism, makes flat jokes on the topic, says that it is a haven for charlatans and "nuts".

And finally, a very recent example that I encountered just a few weeks ago. I relocated from Minsk to Warsaw. Together with my colleague, I officially registered a firm, opened bank accounts, wrote Regulations (an analogue of a public offer agreement) and posted on the website the rules for processing personal data that are required by the EU countries. But when we wanted to connect a payment system to the site, after a month of beating around the bush, we received several refusals with the following wording: "The security policy of our payment system considers payment for esoteric services with bank cards unreliable." Only by the seventh system we tried did everything work, but, as they say, the experience left an aftertaste.

In all these situations there is always a mixture of three very distinct but unpleasant feelings—the triplet of fear, shame and rage. It is these feelings that are most often noted by victims of discrimination. It is important to dwell on each of these feelings in order to delve deeper into the topic.

The fear is understandable. At our workplace, we are brave, since it is "our jurisdiction". If a client comes to us, then they have recognised us as an interlocutor. The client can then devalue us, but it doesn't hit us so hard because we know why he does it. But if we find ourselves in a "big society", we suddenly begin to understand that we are in the minority. And who knows what will happen if we start talking openly about our otherness? Society is not particularly tolerant, and the experience of other minorities suggests that you can run into serious aggression. In addition, purely historically, the fear of a large and cruel inquisition is rooted in us. And the crowd does not need much agitation to begin to shout out the usual: "Burn the witch!" Of course, today, no one will burn anyone, but aggression has so many disguises that it is not always possible to evade it in time.

With a sense of shame, everything is more complicated. This is one of the most toxic feelings, and it is formed in the human psyche very early. It is generally accepted that shame is the feeling of "I am bad", in contrast to guilt, which arises from the feeling of "I did something bad". I, however, prefer the explanation given to me by my psychotherapy teachers. Shame isn't really about "I'm bad". It is more correct to say that this is the feeling of "I don't know what I am". "I'm bad" is more about depressive characterology, while shame pulls our narcissistic strings. In some spheres, we are given a lot of feedback, and there will be no shame, since we know what we are in this topic. Where there is shame, there is a chronic deficit of reflection. It arises when we are given very little or no feedback on a topic. That is why children unconsciously prefer harsh treatment to being completely ignored. The second is much scarier.

Well, how can esotericists not feel shame? Who can give us adequate feedback? The name itself suggests that the "big society" cannot and will not be able to correctly reflect us because we are scholars of the unseen. You can be correctly reflected only in the eyes of your own kind, and esotericists are all so different. That image of the esotericist which has spread through the "big society" is some kind of caricature, a cliché. We are not like that, and we don't want to be seen through such a distorted stereotype! But public opinion has already been formed. Worst of all, I, as an individual, can do nothing about the reputation of esotericism in general. So much empty hype, real quackery and simply monstrous incompetence is in the profession! It's embarrassing not only because we lack professional feedback, but also because our professional identity is heavily stigmatised, and rightfully so. But no matter how much one person shouts that esotericism is not about this, they fail to shout down the majority.

And then there is rage. Rage at unscrupulous and incompetent colleagues. Fury at hypocritical clients who secretly come to consultations while cursing us out loud in wider society. Rage at scientism, the attitude that only scientific knowledge is true. Fury at the militant scientists who seek to test us for insanity in their laboratories. Fury at media, which in its presentation of esotericism constantly oscillates between *X-Men* and *One Flew Over the Cuckoo's Nest*. And this amount of rage, without the ability to channel it, always ends in impotence. This is how our psyche works. A baby left to scream for hours sooner or later falls asleep, as his nervous system is exhausted.

Being the object of discrimination is very difficult. Being a minority in a society where there is not enough tolerance is also not easy. However, calls for some collective activity in the esoteric community do not work. We are too individualistic. It is unlikely that we will arrange our own analogue of a gay pride parade to demand respect and equal rights. It is unlikely that we will stop those who profit from our profession. But what then to do?

We could become the majority and dictate the standards ourselves. And then esotericism would begin to sound everywhere, wherever possible. The "crazy popularisation" of the system begins. Only when it spreads, it spreads like a cancer. The payment for such an active and thoughtless conversion of everyone you meet into a tarologist, astrologer or magician is a terrible profanation of the system. And even if such growth occurred completely unconsciously, the effect of it would only worsen. It becomes even more scary, more shameful, and the rage only grows.

It seems that we still need to take an example from other minorities and adapt their approach to our specifics. The main tool here, in my opinion, is education. We live in a stunningly esoterically incompetent society. If the main goal is to make money, then the dumber the client, the better. In this society, we will continue to be a rejected minority. But a client whose curiosity and informed consent are respected is a huge opportunity for the future. Do not be lazy; you need to answer all the client's most "stupid" questions about what we do. The client is both scared and curious. It can also be said that when many clients contact us, they experience the same emotional triplet—fear, shame and rage. It is necessary to answer their questions and explain these processes because: the more knowledge and understanding, the less fear, shame and rage.

Trust cannot be built once and for all. It will have to be built from scratch with each new client. Do not be offended if they do not trust you, having barely crossed your threshold. Why should a client trust you? This is the first time they're seeing you, and the reputation of the profession, let me remind you, is terrible. You need to win the trust of each individual client. And trust should not be confused with admiration. You can delight in arranging a parade of miracles for the client. But they won't respect you for it. At first, they will admire, then they will be afraid, then they will begin to hate. When you speak honestly with a client about the possibilities and limitations in the profession, and really think about not harming them and respecting them as a person—no matter what "psychopathic horse" they ride to you—the client will also respect and trust you. They may not love and admire you, but they will see you as their equal. And it is very difficult to stigmatise your equal.

We take money for work, so we must comply with the law. Therefore, as it should be, our "product" must have "specifications", or accompanying documents, which clearly describe what kind of product it is. Is it impossible with esotericism? Perhaps, but we can be honest about what we know for sure, and what we have not yet figured out. It is important for the client to know who you are, what you do, and what you can and cannot do, and this information must be true and not false advertising. Of course, this requires work, to sit down and write down your service in detail, as lawyers do. Prescribe the conditions, risks, opportunities, money-back rules, criteria for high-quality and low-quality work. The more transparent we are, the less fear we cause.

"But in this way, we will bury the very spirit of esotericism!!!" I do not think so. In order to study what is happening beyond the veil of the material and subtle worlds, it is not at all necessary to blow fog over your professional image. For me, any professional looks like a magician, whether they're a surgeon or a virtuoso musician. It would take me years to understand what they do and how they do it. They are admired not at all because of the vagueness of their image, but because of their professionalism. Can't it be so in esotericism? Is it easy to learn astrology? Is it so easy to master tarot? You won't see ads for "Training in Neurosurgery in 3 Weeks" anywhere, but in esotericism, such ads are still present. And it is in the power of each individual esotericist who cherishes the reputation of the profession not to profane their work by agreeing to an easy and quick income, to the detriment of quality. Clients need to know where the truth is and where the quackery is.

Returning to the comparison with gay pride, it seems that it begins with one's own practice. This is where we demonstrate the image and quality of our own work that corresponds to the internal ideal of the standard, regardless of what trends exist around. The worst thing happens when the majority begins to crush the minority, forgetting about its uniqueness. After all, avoiding discrimination is not at all an attempt to make everyone the same; it is respect for differences and equal rights and obligations for everyone. If they adhere to responsibility, respect for others and the highest standards of quality for their own work, only then can esotericists truly become a respected minority, with all the rights due to them. And if you know a "witch" personally, and you know how much she studied to work at this level, and you know that she is the same as you, only with competence in a different area, and you know that she respects you and will not do you harm, since she has an ethic that you can understand, then somehow you will feel less like shouting in chorus, "Burn the witch!"

# CONCLUSION

Well, we've reached the end of the first book. I really hope that the information that we've discussed was interesting. These are topics that are rarely covered in books on tarot, but they are directly related to the work of a tarologist. We have only touched on some topics, and I still have a lot of interesting things to tell you.

To pique your interest a little, I invite you to take a look at the Structure Plan of the Series, which you will find on the next page. There you can find out what topics and problematic issues are yet to come, later in the series.

I must say right away that you can read these books in any order. The information does not have a strict sequence, except perhaps in Emma's story. Moreover, many especially important topics I will cover several times. They can be difficult to understand at first, so sometimes you have to return to them, only in a slightly different context.

In my opinion, the modern tarot reader really lacks postgraduate support for their own practice. This is what in classical psychotherapy is called supervision. My colleagues and I are just starting to promote the idea of supervision among tarot readers. But we already have international online groups in which tarologists from different countries gather to talk about difficult moments in their practice, discuss interesting cases, share experiences and receive collegial support. If you are interested in participating in such projects, I would like to invite you there.

I am open to feedback. You can write to me at ghenabel@gmail.com to ask questions, share your impressions or sign up for supervisory groups. You will also find a lot of interesting information about my research projects on my Facebook page, "Henadzi Bialiauski Pro".

See you in the next book in this series.

# PSYCHOLOGY FOR TAROT READERS

## CONTENT OF THE SERIES

| BOOK # 1. PASSIONATE FIRE OF WANDS | | |
|---|---|---|
| SECTION 1. ZODIAC | | |
| Queen of Wands – Aries | King of Wands – Leo | Knight of Wands – Sagittarius |
| SECTION 2. VIGNETTE | | |
| *Empress Takes off her Crown* Chapter 1 | *Empress Takes off her Crown* Chapter 3 | *Empress Takes off her Crown* Chapter 5 |
| SECTION 3. CHARACTEROLOGY | | |
| The Manic Character | The Narcissistic Character | The Histrionic Character |
| SECTION 4. CORE TERM | | |
| Transference and Countertransference | Regression | Triangulation |
| SECTION 5. THEORETICAL LECTURE | | |
| Psychosomatics | Art Therapy | Sexology |
| SECTION 6. USEFUL TERMS | | |
| Character – Accentuation – Psychopathy | Mother – Father – Sibling Figure | Libido – Eros – Thanatos |
| Organismic Valuing<br>Acting Out<br>Zeigarnik Effect<br>Empathy<br>Mentalisation | Narcissistic Expansion<br>Identity<br>Self-Aggression<br>Projection<br>Sublimation | Oedipus Complex<br>Sexualisation<br>Perversions<br>Erotic Transference<br>Reaction Formation |

| SECTION 7. REFLECTION ON A PRACTICAL CASE | | |
|---|---|---|
| *Empress Takes off her Crown* Chapter 2 | *Empress Takes off her Crown* Chapter 4 | *Empress Takes off her Crown* Chapter 6 |
| **SECTION 8. PRACTICAL RECOMMENDATIONS** | | |
| Practical Analysis of Chapters 1 & 2 | Practical Analysis of Chapters 3 & 4 | Practical Analysis of Chapters 5 & 6 |
| **SECTION 9. TRAPS AND DANGERS** | | |
| Absence of Preliminary Instruction | Realising the Limitations in the Work of the Tarot Reader | Psychosomatics: A Scientific and Esoteric View |
| **SECTION – 10. PSYCHOLOGICAL PARADIGM** | | |
| The Psychodynamic Paradigm | Transactional Analysis | The Existential Paradigm |
| **SECTION 11. ESOTERIC ESSAY** | | |
| Anthropomorphic Idea of Higher Forces | The Narcissistic Esotericism of Modernity | Sex and Esotericism |
| **SECTION 12. PROBLEMS OF THE TAROT COMMUNITY** | | |
| Criteria for Competent Tarot Consultation | The Role of the Tarologist in the Client's Life | From Inquisition to Discrimination |

<table>
<tr><th colspan="3">BOOK # 2.<br>RESISTANT EARTH OF PENTACLES</th></tr>
<tr><th colspan="3">SECTION 1. ZODIAC</th></tr>
<tr><td>King of Pentacles –<br>Taurus</td><td>Knight of Pentacles –<br>Virgo</td><td>Queen of Pentacles –<br>Capricorn</td></tr>
<tr><th colspan="3">SECTION 2. VIGNETTE</th></tr>
<tr><td>Empress Takes off her Crown<br>Chapter 7</td><td>Empress Takes off her Crown<br>Chapter 9</td><td>Empress Takes off her Crown<br>Chapter 11</td></tr>
<tr><th colspan="3">SECTION 3. CHARACTEROLOGY</th></tr>
<tr><td>The Oral Character</td><td>The Obsessive-Compulsive Character</td><td>The Paranoid Character</td></tr>
<tr><th colspan="3">SECTION 4. CORE TERM</th></tr>
<tr><td>Developmental Crisis</td><td>Defence Mechanisms</td><td>Aggression</td></tr>
<tr><th colspan="3">SECTION 5. THEORETICAL LECTURE</th></tr>
<tr><td>Developmental Psychology</td><td>Body-Oriented Therapy</td><td>Group Dynamics</td></tr>
<tr><th colspan="3">SECTION 6. USEFUL TERMS</th></tr>
<tr><td>Neurotic –<br>Borderline –<br>Psychotic</td><td>Egotism –<br>Intellectualisation –<br>Alexithymia</td><td>Clarification –<br>Confrontation –<br>Interpretation</td></tr>
<tr><td>Resistance<br>Proflexion<br>Needs<br>Maslow's Pyramid<br>Introjection</td><td>Denial<br>Splitting<br>Omnipotent Control<br>Projective Identification<br>Suppression</td><td>Assertiveness<br>Psychological Violence<br>Conflict<br>Delinquent Behaviour<br>Stigmatisation</td></tr>
<tr><th colspan="3">SECTION 7.<br>REFLECTION ON A PRACTICAL CASE</th></tr>
<tr><td>Empress Takes off her Crown<br>Chapter 8</td><td>Empress Takes off her Crown<br>Chapter 10</td><td>Empress Takes off her Crown<br>Chapter 12</td></tr>
<tr><th colspan="3">SECTION 8.<br>PRACTICAL RECOMMENDATIONS</th></tr>
<tr><td>Practical Analysis of Chapters 7 & 8</td><td>Practical Analysis of Chapters 9 & 10</td><td>Practical Analysis of Chapters 11 & 12</td></tr>
</table>

| SECTION 9. TRAPS AND DANGERS | | |
|---|---|---|
| Mystification of Tarot Practice | Decks, Rituals, Approaches to Tarot | Safety in Esoteric Counselling |
| **SECTION – 10. PSYCHOLOGICAL PARADIGM** | | |
| The Narrative Paradigm | The Cognitive Paradigm | The Behavioural Paradigm |
| **SECTION 11. ESOTERIC ESSAY** | | |
| On Spiritual Teachers and Parental Transference | Pre-Rational and Post-Rational Esotericism | Balance of Frustration and Support |
| **SECTION 12. PROBLEMS OF THE TAROT COMMUNITY** | | |
| How Exactly Do Tarot Cards Work? | Tarot and Science-Oriented Approach | A Question of Professional Esoteric Communities |

| BOOK # 3.<br>RATIONAL AIR OF SWORDS | | |
|---|---|---|
| **SECTION 1. ZODIAC** | | |
| Knight of Swords – Gemini | Queen of Swords – Libra | King of Swords – Aquarius |
| **SECTION 2. VIGNETTE** | | |
| *Empress Takes off her Crown*<br>Chapter 13 | *Empress Takes off her Crown*<br>Chapter 15 | *Empress Takes off her Crown*<br>Chapter 17 |
| **SECTION 3. CHARACTEROLOGY** | | |
| The Symbiotic Character | The Depressive Character | The Dissociative Character |
| **SECTION 4. CORE TERM** | | |
| Egosyntonic and Egodystonic States | Psychological Boundaries | Psychological Norm |
| **SECTION 5. THEORETICAL LECTURE** | | |
| Attachment Theory | Family Therapy | Psychological Trauma |
| **SECTION 6. USEFUL TERMS** | | |
| Psychology –<br>Psychotherapy –<br>Psychiatry | Schizoid –<br>Narcissistic –<br>Neurotic Support | Intercultural Sensitivity –<br>Ethnocentrism –<br>Ethnorelativism |
| Locus of Control<br>Awareness<br>Deflection<br>Phenomenology<br>Diagnostics | Intersection of Contexts<br>Professional Deformation<br>Loyalty to Family<br>Separation<br>Suicidal Behaviour | Awakening Experience<br>EMDR<br>Stockholm Syndrome<br>5 Stages of Grief<br>Debriefing |
| **SECTION 7.<br>REFLECTION ON A PRACTICAL CASE** | | |
| *Empress Takes off her Crown*<br>Chapter 14 | *Empress Takes off her Crown*<br>Chapter 16 | *Empress Takes off her Crown*<br>Chapter 18 |

<table>
<tr><th colspan="3">SECTION 8.<br>PRACTICAL RECOMMENDATIONS</th></tr>
<tr><td>Practical Analysis of Chapters 13 & 14</td><td>Practical Analysis of Chapters 15 & 16</td><td>Practical Analysis of Chapters 17 & 18</td></tr>
<tr><th colspan="3">SECTION 9. TRAPS AND DANGERS</th></tr>
<tr><td>Infantilisation of the Client</td><td>List of Forbidden Topics and Questions</td><td>Possession and Introjection</td></tr>
<tr><th colspan="3">SECTION 10. PSYCHOLOGICAL PARADIGM</th></tr>
<tr><td>The Adlerian Paradigm</td><td>The Systems Paradigm</td><td>The Gender- and Culture-Sensitive Paradigm</td></tr>
<tr><th colspan="3">SECTION 11. ESOTERIC ESSAY</th></tr>
<tr><td>Esotericism as Psychological Compensation</td><td>Identification and Murder of the Personality</td><td>Teenage Opposition to the World</td></tr>
<tr><th colspan="3">SECTION 12.<br>PROBLEMS OF THE TAROT COMMUNITY</th></tr>
<tr><td>The Problem of Conceptualisation in Esotericism</td><td>The Role of Esoteric Discourse in Modern Society</td><td>The Problem of Control and Trust</td></tr>
</table>

<table>
<tr><th colspan="3">BOOK # 4.<br>SENSITIVE WATER OF CUPS</th></tr>
<tr><th colspan="3">SECTION 1. ZODIAC</th></tr>
<tr><td>Queen of Cups –<br>Cancer</td><td>King of Cups –<br>Scorpio</td><td>Knight of Cups –<br>Pisces</td></tr>
<tr><th colspan="3">SECTION 2. VIGNETTE</th></tr>
<tr><td>Empress Takes off her Crown<br>Chapter 19</td><td>Empress Takes off her Crown<br>Chapter 21</td><td>Empress Takes off her Crown<br>Chapter 23</td></tr>
<tr><th colspan="3">SECTION 3. CHARACTEROLOGY</th></tr>
<tr><td>The Schizoid Character</td><td>The Antisocial Character</td><td>The Masochistic Character</td></tr>
<tr><th colspan="3">SECTION 4. CORE TERM</th></tr>
<tr><td>Meta-Position</td><td>Contact</td><td>Magical Thinking</td></tr>
<tr><th colspan="3">SECTION 5. THEORETICAL LECTURE</th></tr>
<tr><td>Dreams and Altered States of Consciousness</td><td>Psychiatry</td><td>Addictions</td></tr>
<tr><th colspan="3">SECTION 6. USEFUL TERMS</th></tr>
<tr><td>Setting –<br>Holding –<br>Containing</td><td>Annihilation –<br>Castration –<br>Separation Anxiety</td><td>Co-Dependency –<br>Counter-Dependency –<br>Inter-Dependency</td></tr>
<tr><td>Free Associations<br>Delusional States<br>Insight<br>Transference Potential<br>Holotropic Breathwork</td><td>Clinical Depression<br>Schizophrenia<br>Eating Disorders<br>Panic Attacks<br>Phobias</td><td>Munchausen Syndrome<br>Twelve-Step Program<br>Field Theory<br>Systemic Constellations<br>Trainings</td></tr>
<tr><th colspan="3">SECTION 7.<br>REFLECTION ON A PRACTICAL CASE</th></tr>
<tr><td>Empress Takes off her Crown<br>Chapter 20</td><td>Empress Takes off her Crown<br>Chapter 22</td><td>Empress Takes off her Crown<br>Chapter 24</td></tr>
<tr><th colspan="3">SECTION 8.<br>PRACTICAL RECOMMENDATIONS</th></tr>
<tr><td>Practical Analysis of Chapters 19 & 20</td><td>Practical Analysis of Chapters 21 & 22</td><td>Practical Analysis of Chapters 23 & 24</td></tr>
</table>

| SECTION 9. TRAPS AND DANGERS | | |
|---|---|---|
| Money and Other Elements of Setting | The Topic of Death in Esotericism and Psychology | Four Types of Dangerous Clients |
| **SECTION 10. PSYCHOLOGICAL PARADIGM** | | |
| The Person-Centred Paradigm | The Gestalt Paradigm | The Jungian Paradigm |
| **SECTION 11. ESOTERIC ESSAY** | | |
| About Sacrifice and Its Interpretations | Hexing in Tarot Consulting | A Subtle Schizoid Veil of Esotericism |
| **SECTION 12. PROBLEMS OF THE TAROT COMMUNITY** | | |
| Is a Standard Possible in Esoteric Development? | Prospects for Cooperation of Esotericism and Psychiatry | Prospects for the Development of the World Tarot |

# TAROT INDEX

In this table you will find the names of the Tarot arcana in the upright and reversed position, as well as the page numbers in the book on which this card is mentioned or is associated with the content of the text.

| NAME OF ARCANA | UPRIGHT POSITION | REVERSED POSITION |
|---|---|---|
| THE FOOL | 33, 58, 59, 164, 216 | 36, 131 |
| THE MAGICIAN | 45, 64, 165 | 20, 24, 35, 118, 182, 192 |
| THE HIGH PRIESTESS | 48, 63, 132, 135, 185 | 44, 50, 195, 199, 218 |
| THE EMPRESS | 28, 123, 130, 134, 219 | 48, 141 |
| THE EMPEROR | 40, 108, 193, 196 | 20, 137 |
| THE HIEROPHANT | 83, 136, 140, 161, 165, 208 | 164, 218, 234 |
| THE LOVERS | 82, 201, 204, 213, 236 | 145, 189, 195, 206 |
| THE CHARIOT | 26, 65, 117 | 86, 122 |
| STRENGTH | 38, 62, 84, 135, 142, 208 | 50, 124, 192, 216 |
| THE HERMIT | 47, 111, 142, 237 | 144 |
| WHEEL OF FORTUNE | 37, 46, 116, 164, 210 | 61, 119, 122 |
| JUSTICE | 85, 200 | 41, 60, 210 |
| THE HANGED MAN | 25, 45, 62, 127, 212, 220 | 38, 120 |
| DEATH | 53, 143, 212, 235 | |
| TEMPERANCE | 49, 115, 120, 127, 146, 207 | 41 |
| THE DEVIL | 34, 65, 108, 140, 141, 192, 217 | 146, 182 |
| THE TOWER | 34, 121 | 203 |
| THE STAR | 54, 134 | 43 |

| | | |
|---|---|---|
| THE MOON | 39, 51, 57, 84, 118, 190, 197 | 163, 211 |
| THE SUN | 33, 59, 136, 139 | 55 |
| JUDGEMENT | 83, 114, 132, 162 | |
| THE WORLD | 39, 55, 128, 198, 211 | |
| | | |
| Ace of Wands | 32, 209 | 216 |
| 2 of Wands | 236 | 35, 206 |
| 3 of Wands | 144 | 219 |
| 4 of Wands | 108 | |
| 5 of Wands | 62, 84, 117 | |
| 6 of Wands | 38, 116, 119 | 108 |
| 7 of Wands | 52, 59, 185, 220 | |
| 8 of Wands | 199 | 65, 145 |
| 9 of Wands | 85, 202 | |
| 10 of Wands | | |
| Page of Wands | 32, 114, 161 | 37, 182 |
| Knight of Wands | 173 | 175 |
| Queen of Wands | 12 | 14 |
| King of Wands | 99, 193 | 101 |
| | | |
| Ace of Pentacles | 56, 108, 131, 211 | |
| 2 of Pentacles | 35, 56, 147 | 185 |
| 3 of Pentacles | 58, 82, 87, 142, 198 | 108 |
| 4 of Pentacles | 53, 108, 218 | |
| 5 of Pentacles | 111 | |
| 6 of Pentacles | | 119 |
| 7 of Pentacles | 108 | 219 |
| 8 of Pentacles | 20, 83, 137, 200 | 50 |
| 9 of Pentacles | 139 | 117 |
| 10 of Pentacles | 53, 115, 134, 181 | 141 |
| Page of Pentacles | 47, 126, 129, 181 | |
| Knight of Pentacles | 46, 185, 203, 235 | |
| Queen of Pentacles | 143 | |
| King of Pentacles | 42, 237 | |
| | | |

| Ace of Swords | 38, 209 | |
|---|---|---|
| 2 of Swords | 33 | |
| 3 of Swords | 40, 136, 199 | |
| 4 of Swords | 31, 122 | 60 |
| 5 of Swords | 40, 116, 145, 181 | |
| 6 of Swords | 25, 34, 234 | |
| 7 of Swords | 46, 143, 191 | |
| 8 of Swords | 43, 51, 108 | |
| 9 of Swords | 42, 64, 124 | 125 |
| 10 of Swords | 25, 63 | 237 |
| Page of Swords | 129 | |
| Knight of Swords | 220 | |
| Queen of Swords | 221 | 215 |
| King of Swords | 125, 162 | 144, 181, 214 |
| | | |
| Ace of Cups | 85 | 41 |
| 2 of Cups | 48, 64, 108, 123, 146, 205 | 147, 163, 182, 193 |
| 3 of Cups | 138, 161, 194, 197 | 162, 198 |
| 4 of Cups | 37, 49, 218 | 60 |
| 5 of Cups | 33, 56, 137, 235 | |
| 6 of Cups | 61, 111, 129, 187 | 125 |
| 7 of Cups | 20, 30, 130, 204 | |
| 8 of Cups | 108 | |
| 9 of Cups | 108, 124 | 36 |
| 10 of Cups | 205, 214 | 42, 219 |
| Page of Cups | 58, 139, 215 | 32, 63, 190 |
| Knight of Cups | 128 | 189 |
| Queen of Cups | 51, 64 | 43 |
| King of Cups | 133 | 37 |

# RECOMMENDED READING


1. Barry Weinhold, Janae B. Weinhold. *Breaking Free of the Co-Dependency Trap.*
2. Bessel van der Kolk. *The Body Keeps the Score: Brain, Mind, and Body in the Healing of Trauma.*
3. Carl Jung. *Psychology of the Unconscious.*
4. David M. Buss. *The Evolution of Desire: Strategies of Human Mating.*
5. Douglas Kenrick, Steven L. Neuberg, et al. *Social Psychology: Goals in Interaction.*
6. Eric Bern. *Games People Play.*
7. Frans De Waal. *The Bonobo and the Atheist: In Search of Humanism Among the Primates.*
8. Gary Chapman. *The 5 Love Languages.The Secret of Love That Lasts.*
9. Grace J. Craig, Don Baucum. *Human Development.*
10. James Hollis. *Swamplands of Soul: New Life in Dismal Places.*
11. Irvin D. Yalom, Molyn Leszcz. *The Theory and Practice of Group Psychotherapy.*
12. Irvin D. Yalom. *Staring at the Sun: Overcoming the Terror of Death.*
13. James Hollis. *The Middle Passage from Misery to Meaning in Mid-Life.*
14. James Hollis. *Under Saturn's Shadow: The Wounding and Healing of Men.*
15. James O. Prochaska, John C. Norcross. *Systems of Psychotherapy.*
16. Jerome S. Blackman. *Get the Diagnosis Right: Assessment and Treatment Selection for Mental Disorders.*
17. Karl Heinz Brisch. *Treating Attachment Disorder.*

18. Larry Hjelle, Daniel Ziegler. *Personality Theories: Basic Assumptions, Research, and Applications.*
19. Michael Gelder, Nancy Andreasen, Juan Lopez-Ibor, John Geddes. *New Oxford Textbook of Psychiatry.*
20. Nancy McWilliams. *Psychoanalytic Case Formulation.*
21. Nancy McWilliams. *Psychoanalytic Diagnosis.*
22. Otto F. Kernberg. *Severe Personality Disorders: Psychotherapeutic Strategies.*
23. Peter A. Levine. *Waking the Tiger: Healing Trauma.*
24. R. Horacio Etchegoyen. *Fundamentals of Psychoanalytic Technique.*
25. Robert M. Sapolsky. *Why Zebras Don't Get Ulcers.*
26. Ronald Comer. *Fundamentals of Abnormal Psychology.*
27. Stephen M. Johnson Ph. D. *Character Styles.*

# AUTHOR PROFILE

Henadzi Bialiauski is a tarologist, astrologer and psychologist from Minsk, Belarus, who currently lives and works in Warsaw, Poland. With more than 20 years of experience in the fields of Tarot cards and astrology, as well as traditional training in the fields of psychotherapy and scientific psychology, he relies on a scientifically oriented approach and interdisciplinarity when considering topics such as Tarot cards and astrology, conducting research, teaching, and writing books. This is his fifth book, but his first in English.

In the course of his research, he found that modern tarologists are very lacking in psychological knowledge, as well as support in organizing their own counselling practice. This series of books aims to fill this gap by offering fellow tarologists the opportunity to look at their Tarot practice from the point of view of classical psychology and psychotherapy.

https://group-bial.com/en/
https://www.instagram.com/belgroup9/
https://www.facebook.com/groups/1319183008930656

## What Did You Think of
## *Psychology for Tarot Readers: Passionate Fire of Wands?*

*A big thank you for purchasing this book. It means a lot that you chose this book specifically from such a wide range on offer. I do hope you enjoyed it.*

*Book reviews are incredibly important for an author. All feedback helps them improve their writing for future projects and for developing this edition. If you are able to spare a few minutes to post a review on Amazon, that would be much appreciated.*

Publisher Information

Rowanvale Books provides publishing services to independent authors, writers and poets all over the globe. We deliver a personal, honest and efficient service that allows authors to see their work published, while remaining in control of the process and retaining their creativity. By making publishing services available to authors in a cost-effective and ethical way, we at Rowanvale Books hope to ensure that the local, national and international community benefits from a steady stream of good quality literature.

For more information about us, our authors or our publications, please get in touch.

www.rowanvalebooks.com
info@rowanvalebooks.com

www.ingramcontent.com/pod-product-compliance
Ingram Content Group UK Ltd.
Pitfield, Milton Keynes, MK11 3LW, UK
UKHW062303290726
14090UKWH00017B/869